Understanding Transference

Understanding Transference

The Power of Patterns in the Therapeutic Relationship

Lesley Murdin
Director, WPF Therapy

Consultant Editor: *Ann Scott*

First published 2010 by
PALGRAVE MACMILLAN

Palgrave Macmillan in the UK is an imprint of Macmillan Publishers Limited,
registered in England, company number 785998, of Houndmills, Basingstoke,
Hampshire RG21 6XS.

Palgrave Macmillan in the US is a division of St Martin's Press LLC,
175 Fifth Avenue, New York, NY 10010.

Palgrave Macmillan is the global academic imprint of the above companies
and has companies and representatives throughout the world.

Palgrave® and Macmillan® are registered trademarks in the United States,
the United Kingdom, Europe and other countries.

ISBN 978-1-4039-2118-5

This book is printed on paper suitable for recycling and made from fully
managed and sustained forest sources. Logging, pulping and manufacturing
processes are expected to conform to the environmental regulations of the
country of origin.

A catalogue record for this book is available from the British Library.

A catalog record for this book is available from the Library of Congress.

10   9   8   7   6   5   4   3   2   1
19 18 17 16 15 14 13 12 11 10

Printed in Great Britain by
CPI Antony Rowe, Chippenham and Eastbourne

This book is dedicated to my sisters, Jane and Patricia and to my mother.

Contents

Foreword

Psychotherapy, at least in the UK, has traditionally been taught on an apprenticeship model. It is, in addition, a tenet of analytic psychotherapy that change comes through working through in the transference. But what does this mean in practice, and what does it mean in non-intensive as well as intensive psychotherapy? Starting from the position that trainees need to develop both craft and conceptual skill, Lesley Murdin deconstructs the building-blocks of transference work. The book starts with the experience of teaching and is intended to be a text for teaching and learning. Murdin has a wealth of experience as a teacher of trainee counsellors and psychotherapists; as she says, 'The text imitates a therapeutic session which is a catalyst for thought and emotional processes that go on after it is finished'. She brings to the discussion her evocative and intuitive grasp of the clinical situation, and her wealth of experience as a clinician with a working knowledge of Freudian, Jungian, Lacanian and person-centred approaches to conceptualization and intervention.

It is in the nature of open-ended psychodynamic work – as distinct from, say, cognitive behavioural therapy – that the aim of the individual session is relatively if not completely unspecified. The arc of change is not prescribed. To be able to trace and use patterns in the clinical context therefore requires considerable skill. In particular, Murdin offers an engagement with the experience of the developing clinician in teasing out the relative ease of working, say, with one type of transference rather than another, especially where the therapist is, as is often the case, a woman. And just as analytic supervision centres on the presentation of verbatim material, with the supervisor considering what might have been said differently, so Murdin engages the reader in a detailed consideration of possible interventions with hindsight. Her clinical language is ordinary, everyday and vivid. She does not shy away from looking at therapist errors. It is, after all, very easy for a therapist to get into difficulty over managing her own anger, with an angry patient. Questions of self-revelation pose particular demands in terms of technique and ethics, especially if a therapist is faced with a difficulty in her actual situation, as occurs in serious illness.

Psychotherapists now are increasingly familiar – however ambivalently – with the principles of evidence-based practice. Murdin extends the theme of evidence to the idea of 'evidence-based living', seeing the therapist's task as a slow and steady unpicking of the patient's habitual responses, working with their transference roots and standing for the principle of a new and more free way of living. At the same time, she recognises that truth is always provisional and that no one way of telling one's story can ever be complete. There will be a multiplicity of narratives. It is for the patient and therapist, working together step-by-step, to identify the narrative that holds most transformative power for the patient. However, the emphasis on narrative is not unbounded. There is a firm advocacy of familiarity with key features of developmental biology and key symptoms of, say, brain disease, to enable the therapist to recognise something that is out of the developmental path for the individual.

Even as her central focus remains psychoanalytic, the pluralist respect that Murdin brings to the consulting room is complemented by her understanding that analytic work is now operating in a multi-modality therapeutic culture. Analytic thinking, with its fine-grained attention to individual, subjective experience, has to find a relevant place for itself in a postmodern world in which specific religious fundamentalisms coexist with a global, internet-based way of relating. As computer-based cognitive behavioural therapy expands, and health care systems in the West appear minded to support non-intensive psychotherapy, so there may be a reduction in demand for intensive analytic treatment, and 'the need will be to train trainees to work carefully and responsibly with transference in once-weekly therapy'. None of this detracts from the continuing relevance of psychoanalytic clinical formulation, or the relevance of continuing debate about psychoanalytic education. Psychotherapy and counselling trainees are often extremely interested in the politics of their profession and Murdin speaks, unusually and democratically, to trainees as well as qualified therapists in addressing issues about training and transference. She considers the pro's and con's of a Lacanian system of self-authorization, setting them against the more usual hierarchical systems of judgement and readiness to qualify. It will be through transparency and reflective thinking of this kind that the profession will develop the capacity to hold a space for analytic thinking, and to engage in internal, collegial debate about the most effective way to move forward in the work.

Ann Scott
Member, British Association of Psychotherapists
Editor, *British Journal of Psychotherapy*

Acknowledgements

I should like to thank all my patients and supervisees for all that they have taught me and of course, most of all, my own therapist and supervisors.

I have been given help and advice by Meg Errington and I am profoundly grateful for her wisdom and experience which she has generously allowed me to share.

Stephen Crawford, Mary Anne Coate and Lynsey Hotchkies gave me valuable advice on the plan for which I am grateful.

The book owes most to the careful and wise editing of Ann Scott and I would like to thank her for her patience and thoughtful help.

Lastly, my thanks to my husband for his help with the manuscript and his helpful and thought provoking comments.

Introduction

The inspiration for this book was my own experience of teaching generations of people to practise analytic therapy. My intention is to offer to both teachers and learners, or perhaps just to learners, because that term includes all of us, an opportunity to think through the rationale for the concepts of transference and counter-transference. Both 'transference' and 'counter-transference' imply patterns – patterns of responding, patterns of understanding. As we know, patterns are important to human perception and to human thinking. Aesthetics and science alike depend on the beauty of patterns and our understanding of when a pattern is formed and when it is broken. Psychoanalysis and its derivatives have analysed the suffering that arises from human experience and have shown that we can be trapped by patterns of thinking, feeling and behaving. Analysing patterns and then using the analysis of patterns can help to relieve suffering and this rationale for therapeutic process is the subject of this book. Although no-one can ever claim to know all there is to know about himself, never mind about other people, and learning about how we function is a life long enterprise, such learning can be helped by a better understanding of the transference patterns through which we all interact with the outside world and with each other. With an understanding of the theory, we can approach its practical use to ease suffering and enable people to choose to live their lives more fully and more consciously.

The work of Sigmund Freud provides the bedrock of the theoretical orientation of the book. Although he was not the first to see the importance of the unconscious functioning of the mind, he was the writer who set out the relevance of this concept for understanding the habitual functioning of the wish that underlies a neurotic symptom and its roots in the experience of the long forgotten past. Many people found that Freud spoke to them of what they already half knew. In France, André Gide, spoke of having found in Freud *'rather an authorisation than an awakening'*. In Germany, Thomas Mann spoke admiringly of Freud's heroic achievement and of his insight into human nature.

In England, W. H. Auden greeted psychoanalysis enthusiastically, writing of Freud:

> To us he is no more a person
> Now but a whole climate of opinion.

Freud taught us that wishes do not have to be consciously known to be powerful and that, in fact, the more compelling the wish, the more likely it is to be kept from conscious awareness. What is not conscious can still affect the conscious mind. Freud also saw that the fundamental structures in the mind can be described in terms of the myth of Oedipus. The human child has to move over from the sole possession of his mother and give place to his father or to the rest of his mother's life and interests. This surrender provides a theme, a template or a pattern which remains actively structuring the mind of the adult long after the childhood experience has been forgotten. These ideas also structure the thinking in this book.

I make no apology for beginning with Freud. There is considerable anecdotal evidence that a high percentage of therapists trace the origins of their own practice to psychoanalysis and therefore to Freud. Of course, theory has moved on and changed since his seminal works written between 1893 and 1939 but most of the developments have taken his ideas as the starting point and have either reacted against them or developed them further.

Carl Jung separated himself from Freud both as a friend and as a working colleague over the fundamental importance of infantile sexuality. Thanks to him, it became possible to read and use an alternative version of the functioning of the psyche based on the importance of the universal patterns of human emotional experience. These patterns he called *archetypes* and just as the Freudians chase the wishes or desires that drive the motors of human action, so the Jungians also seek the emotional patterns that are driving each individual. I have been influenced by Jung's use of the alchemical metaphor which has enabled me to see more clearly that the transference relationship is in itself transformative and capable of establishing new patterns.

The theoretical base of the book is contemporary Freudian, although my own training and personal therapy was strongly Jungian with a liberal helping from the British Object Relations

School. More recently I have benefited greatly from thinking about the return to Freud that was staged by Jacques Lacan and the French school. The work of Jacques Lacan provides a challenge to accepted ideas and to any complacency about knowing what Freud intended. Lacan's ability to make Freud's thoughts appear in a new light has been an important influence and will feature in this book. Without necessarily agreeing with him even when I think I understand him, I have learned from puzzling over his meaning and over why I might or might not accept his views.

The book also takes account of the Humanistic tradition in relation to an approach to teaching and learning: we do not so much teach as offer an opportunity for people to learn. This applies particularly strongly to psychoanalysis which is lived and experienced, not just learned and reproduced. It demands that the practitioner first acquire it for herself and then, as in many spiritual traditions, can offer to pass it on to those who wish to learn it. This line of thought leads inevitably to the importance of the personal experience of the analytic therapist. The most important learning goes on in the analysis or psychotherapy of the practitioner and a weight of responsibility rests on the shoulders of the training therapist who shows in the heat of the personal therapy how transference patterns matter and how they can be used therapeutically.

Because the book refers to several ways of describing mental functioning, clearly it does not subscribe to any one theory as the truth. In fact, the multiplicity of narratives is taken to be one of the conditions of human life and therefore is one of the challenges and also one of the rewards of therapeutic work. We work in a world in which each person may be able to find a way of describing his experience that is coherent and can therefore be said to be his own truth. This is not intended to imply that there is any one unitary truth or 'theory of everything'. Physicists have not been able to find a mathematical description of the universe yet and it is small wonder that those who seek to account for the development and functioning of the mind have not been able to tie its diversity down in words. *Truth* is therefore recognised to be provisional and not absolute but is the best that we can rely on in the present and is not refuted by any known evidence.

I am writing as a psychoanalytic psychotherapist with experience of training both psychotherapists and counsellors. I shall therefore use the terms *therapist, practitioner* or *clinician* to denote psychoanalysts, psychotherapists, psychologists and counsellors. I shall refer to *patients,* since the word is derived from the Greek verb *to suffer,* rather than to *clients,* which is derived from the Latin *cliens* meaning *dependent.* Analytic therapists are concerned to help their patients to deal with fears of dependency and perhaps arrive at a capacity for mature interdependency with another. I prefer to think of working with people who are suffering rather than with people who will stay dependent. I write of the patient in general with the masculine pronoun and the therapist with the feminine since the majority of therapists, taking account of all three levels of the profession, are women.

I am also well aware of the variety of models of clinical practice available in the twenty first century. In the UK and the US, the vast majority of psychological therapy is carried out once weekly and not at the high intensity of the early practice when people were seen five or even six times per week. These parameters mean that analytic therapy is often practised in a context which is very different from the early days and the model must be correspondingly adapted to the needs of the patients who will be presenting themselves in the consulting room. The gap between once weekly sessions is to be taken into account in the timing of interpretations made in a session. Those who are practising an intensive model, seeing people three, four or five times per week may have the luxury of being able to watch a process unfolding with relatively little external interference.

Because this book is intended to be a text for teaching and learning, I have asked teachers in the field what would be most helpful to them and, as a result I have included a great deal of case material which can be used as the basis of discussion. I have also collected some of the main points of each chapter and formulated them as questions for discussion. I have begun each chapter with a series of questions which the reader should have in mind when reading. In my experience of teaching both beginning and more experienced therapists, I have found that asking them to prepare answers to specific questions, linked with the reading for a seminar, such as those that I have suggested at the beginning of each chapter, is a good preparation for learning. Reading with a questioning attitude is much more likely to be assimilated than reading with no specific purpose. Discussion invariably rises from these points but I have also included some specific discussion points that might be useful for a group to consider. The questioning attitude helps concentration and helps the reader to enter a dialogue with the text which will inevitably fail to satisfy all needs and will require the reader to go beyond what is provided. In this way, the text itself imitates a therapeutic session which is a catalyst for thought and emotional processes that go on after it is finished.

At each stage in the process, we might all stop to ponder the ways in which the understanding of patterns can be applied to clinical practice. For that reason I have included clinical illustrations at many points in the text and vignettes at the end of each chapter. All my illustrations are from published sources or are fictitious compilations derived from work that I have done, in my roles as school psychotherapist, NHS psychotherapist or as a psychotherapist in private practice. Patient confidentiality is of the utmost importance in our work. I have therefore used fictitious case studies. Although they are based in experience, they do not represent any one person's experience. The therapist in supervision and her supervisor are also fictitious but are also derived from experience.

The book, therefore, reflects a progress through patterns of thinking and through the theoretical schools but is mainly, I hope, a distillation of a long period of clinical practice. Chapter 1 examines the theoretical approach to the way in which patterns help us to think about the new experience that we constantly encounter. This chapter gives an introduction to the various uses to which the meaning of the term 'transference' can be put and to its origin in the need of the human mind to make sense of experience. As part of this conceptual framework the book considers fundamental concepts such as the unconscious, mind and the process of change. The overall aim is to show how patterns are used in human interaction.

Chapter 2 goes on to the application of theory to the therapeutic environment. It begins the theoretical discussion of the use of transference as defence and shows how it leads to its mirror image in counter-transference. A basic understanding of the attitude of the main analytic models is introduced to show how they converge or diverge.

Chapter 3 approaches the origins of the patterns that predominates in the adult and asks the reader to consider the effect on the adult patient of the different family relationships to which they will have been subjected. In recent years the attention of writers has turned to the influence of siblings and position in family. We might reasonably expect that the transference patterns of someone with an older brother could have a different quality from those of someone with a younger brother. In spite of some general reflections on the nature of the resulting patterns, the chapter emphasises the importance of the individual and the extent to which individuals will differ.

Chapter 4 has a clinical focus and examines ways in which therapists can use an understanding of the patterns of the past to help people to escape from counter productive cycles of thought and behaviour and move on to facing what is in front of them in the present. Several common technical terms are defined and illustrated, e.g. projection and projective identification.

The nature of the evidence base for analytic therapy is of importance to those who believe that they are engaged in seeking truth. It is also, of course, of great importance to those who have to face the economic costs and realities of offering psychotherapy and counselling in a way that is economically viable. Chapter 5 is concerned with what we know of human development and of the way in which the brain and the mind are either related concepts or are each of a different order. This chapter also addresses the importance of the human achievement of language and its impact on shaping the developing mind of the child and the adult.

Chapter 6 examines the question of cure. Does a therapist seek to cure symptoms? If not, what does analytic therapy seek to achieve? The difficult question of whether the patient and the therapist share a common purpose and whether analytic therapy makes the patient worse are both considered. This chapter also discusses the relevance of the concept of narcissism for both therapist and patient.

Using and interpreting transference patterns can give great psychological power to the therapist. Chapter 7 addresses the questions raised by this power and its use and misuse. The reader is asked to consider the areas of content in therapy which are likely to lead to exploitation or abuse such as sexual relationships. It also raises questions about how the therapist may deal with the temptations and snares of other forms of exploitation and abuse of any sort. The chapter does not purport to give all the answers but does ask the therapist to consider her responsibilities.

Teaching and learning must be processes that are inextricably linked and Chapter 8 looks at the ways in which the patterns of transference affect those who teach and those who learn. It examines the question of whether it is possible to teach analytic work or whether it is something that each person must acquire for herself through her own analytic therapy. The argument is that the process of understanding transference is itself part of the education that needs to be acquired. The conclusion of the book is a resounding affirmation of the value of analytic work and its power to transform neurotic misery into ordinary human happiness as well as to make our ordinary happiness bearable.

1 The Story of Transference

Questions to consider while reading

1. What is *transference*?
2. What brings about change in patterns?
3. What is projection?
4. What part do patterns play in the mind
   - Of the patient?
   - Of the therapist?

Introduction

Why do we need to think in terms of *transference*? 'The past is a foreign country,' wrote the novelist L.P. Hartley in the novel about the child's induction into the world of adult sexuality, *The Go Between* (1953). We may find that we no longer speak the same language and the people have different customs that we no longer understand. But surely the past is no longer relevant? Surely we can leave it behind and forget it? That is perhaps the problem. We cannot always forget it. Even if we do manage to forget our past experience, it leaves traces. Those traces make a difference in the present. That is the reason for the importance of understanding transference patterns. This concept makes psychoanalytically based therapy different from others and puts great emphasis on the therapeutic relationship, where the transference trace will appear like a muddy footprint on a white carpet.

Defn *Transference* as a term in analytic theory and practice refers to the process by which past experiences that an individual has had will be retained in the mind in some form and can

8

later be projected onto a new experience, acting like a kind of coloured filter which changes the appearance of the new experience. This process happens outside of conscious awareness. Because people manage new experience by filtering it through what is familiar, it is a process that occurs everywhere all the time. It therefore appears in the therapeutic relationship and can be seen even in the first encounter or perhaps especially in the first encounter. At that time, there is little evidence of what the other person is like to counteract the transferred assumptions from the past. Therapists always need to remember that transference is a human phenomenon from which they are not exempt and we will always have to try to recognise our own transference to the patient. It is therefore impossible to write about transference without also considering counter-transference. This first chapter will consider the rationale for the therapeutic use of transference patterns and Chapter 2 will consider the use of counter-transference. Both transference and counter-transference will be considered from the basic standpoint of Freud's thinking. The modifications and differences proposed by Carl Jung, Melanie Klein and Jacques Lacan and contemporary writers are also given consideration.

Repetition is Inevitable

Why should transference be helpful to the therapeutic purpose rather than a hindrance as Sigmund Freud first thought that it was? He had seen it as 'the most powerful resistance to the treatment (1912: 101). He came to understand that it could also be a powerful therapeutic tool. The irony is that it can serve both functions at once, both protecting the patient from the reality of the relationship with his therapist and also showing the therapist what the matter is. A very common presenting problem for someone coming to see a therapist is demonstrated by Mr M:

> A young man of 27, Mr M, comes to see a therapist because his boss has said that unless he makes some changes he will lose his job. He works as a mechanic in a car sales room. He feels that his boss, Doug, who is much older, does not understand young people. Doug, he says, comes in sometimes

with a hangover and then: 'He just goes for me. I might have stayed on the night before to finish a job, and will he pay me for overtime? Will he? No way. Once I came in late because I had had a few drinks the night before and got a bit wrecked. He started to have a go at me over something that wasn't right. Then I went for him. I didn't hit him or nothing but I swore at him. He wouldn't take that and I don't know why I did that. It was just stupid but I can't shut up now. Every time I see him it starts to come over me and I want to kill him. Why do I feel that bad? I've got to stop it.'

What will the therapist do to help this man? She might empathise with the feelings that are expressed here. She might encourage the client to say more about his feelings. She might belong to a person centred school of therapy and say 'You need to give yourself permission to express your own feelings'.

That might lead to useful exploration of Mr M's reasons for feeling angry. On the other hand the exploration might reach an impasse in which the patient is aware of the therapist's empathic understanding but is still not able to progress to changing the behaviour which in Mr M's case could lead to a physical assault and perhaps get him into serious trouble.

One approach that might be appropriate would be to refer Mr M to a cognitive behavioural therapist, who might begin immediately to tackle the behaviour itself through the thinking that leads to the rage and offers no alternative. This is one possible response that could well be helpful. On the other hand, an analytic approach could bring some immediate help to the situation. We would apply the basic principle that the effects of the past do not disappear but are still present in the individual's reaction to the world around him. The second principle that we would apply would be the idea that understanding why there is a strong emotional reaction to the boss's behaviour would help Mr M to have the possibility of choosing to modify his behaviour.

Stated like that, both of these concepts might seem clear and uncontroversial. What is the difficulty in accepting that these are the basic principles of psychological change? Many therapists, let alone clients, would like to get on with what seems most urgent at the time. Mr M clearly has urgent problems in dealing with anger and relating well to other people. Why would he agree to mess about with his past? Then again there is the school of thought that says he should pull himself together and just control his temper. Trying to see the roots of his current problem in his past experience invites the mockery that is illustrated in the song of the young gang members in *West Side Story*: 'Dear Officer Krupke, we're misunderstood.' The young people are probably often misunderstood but that cannot be an excuse for delinquent behaviour and the song's cheerfully mocking tone makes clear that trying to make it an excuse is worthy of ridicule. On the other hand, the older generation of any period finds it difficult not to shed a general golden light on the distant past and to believe that everyone and everything is worse now than it used to be before their own physical and mental abilities began to decline. For this reason, older people tend to see accounts of behaviour in the present which relate the behaviour to experience in the individual's past, particularly of young people as excuses: 'They should pull themselves together, make an effort' etc.

So if we expect people to spend many hours and much money sitting on a chair or lying on a couch revisiting experiences that they would probably like to forget (but cannot), we have to have a very good rationale, preferably supported with evidence. We shall begin with the rationale and return to the case of Mr M in Chapter 3.

Patterns Require Continuity

Freud was not the first to think that the past history of an individual would be important in understanding his present difficulties. In *The Unconscious before Freud* L.L. Whyte traced the background to the ideas that Freud put forward in a more integrated theory. He gives importance to the year 1600 because it is at the centre of the period in history when self awareness and reflection on the nature of man and his relationships with others was leading to a new theory of mind. Self awareness was not unique to any period of history but it had different manifestations at different times. The self awareness represented by, for example, Shakespeare and the Renaissance was more closely connected to man's dependence on ideas of God, Fate and Destiny than to the self awareness of the eighteenth century Enlightenment which on the whole elevated the value of human reason and its ability to lead the individual to a better understanding of himself and of the world. All the manifestations of self awareness of which we can conceive, lead us to understand that we are only fitfully aware of ourselves and of our mental processes. Awareness is constantly interrupted by absorption in perceptions coming from the outside or from inside the body itself. During sleep and dreaming are usually also times when self awareness is suspended although there are the so called 'lucid dreams' in which the dreamer is aware that she is dreaming.

The double mirrors that reflect a person's awareness of self awareness show a way to understand that there must be some function that continues when self awareness is not functioning. I know that I am not always aware of myself and my functioning, but am just engaged in the present moment. Something else in me continues and allows me to wake to be more or less the same self again after some sort of absence. Discovering the discontinuities in the human mind leads us to ask more about what enables there to be any continuity. The theory of transference is one of the outcomes of asking this sort of question. The idea that there may be some function that continues out of awareness is of course a way of stating the existence of unconscious functioning. It also leads us to ask questions about the nature of time and its relativity.

Since Descartes in the seventeenth century presented us with the idea that self-awareness is the measure and proof of existence ('*I think therefore I am*'), we have had to deal with the problem of continuity in time. We deal with the twin imperatives: to change and to stay the same. A therapist earns her living by working with the idea that the person who comes to her at six pm on a Wednesday brings essentially the same mind as the person who came at six pm on Wednesday last week. Without some degree of continuity, our hope of understanding the mind of the other would be very small indeed. The body changes all the time. The cells that constitute the body that a person has today will have died and been replaced in a matter of years so that the person is physically in a constant state of flux. Only the brain cells are not replaced. The central

organising function that we can call the *ego* remains sufficiently
the same for there to be some continuity of existence through
consciousness and the analytic therapist would say also through
the unconscious.

Change and Negative Therapeutic Reaction

The therapist is concerned with continuity and what gives to
a person a sense of self or of being a subject and the other
pole of the therapist's concern is change and the creation of a
discontinuity.

The degree of confidence that each person has in the continuity of himself as a subject is the confidence to allow change.
Within the continuity of self in the mind of any individual, the
therapist allows that there will have been changes. Patients who
respond to questions about the process of change often do not
know how they have changed but are able to say only that
change had taken place. Therapists must be optimistic while
remaining neutral about what changes there might be, The therapist hopes that there will have been some changes between
sessions. In this way she has to be mindful of the importance
of not directing the patient towards the therapist's goals and
at the same time she must maintain her belief that she can do
more good than harm to the patient whom she sees. Yet, during a supervision session, the therapist may sometimes express
despair: 'It's the same thing over and over again'. The answer
to this is, of course, that patients need to bring us the same old
thing, until we find the way to enable change to take place. But
change itself is a mystery. What is it that is changing and how do
we know when *it* has changed? The experienced therapist will
not get too excited about one or two changes for the better that
the patient may report but will be listening for her own sort of
indicators of change. These will depend on the theoretical model
that she is following.

The possibility of change is also limited by the phenomenon
of negative therapeutic reaction. Newton's Law of Dynamics
states that every action has an equal and opposite reaction;
the therapist has to accept that for many actions that bring
positive improvements there is an equal and opposite reaction

back to the negative. For most patients there is a good reason not to get better. Most obviously people do not want to
get better because that may mean leaving the therapist who
has begun to matter to an extent that is often not consciously
admitted. Freud examined this phenomenon and concluded that
it was caused by unconscious feelings of guilt which in themselves lead back to the theory of the death drive (1920). The
patient may choose to suffer rather than risk the guilt of being
cured: As long as he suffers he will not be punished further. In
addition, he knows and recognises his familiar present suffering.
This is one of the most important concepts to help us to understand what inhibits change. Other aspects of this tendency to
negate or invalidate changes for the better will be discussed in
Chapter 2.

No matter what her theoretical model, the therapist must be
looking for change. Change may be in patterns of thinking, feeling or behaviour. The patient may stop smoking or may stop
shouting at his wife. This may be all that is required or expected
and for some therapists it will signal time to end the therapy.
What is often called *deeper change* may be change of the mental
structures or patterns. This sort of change means that experiences can be received in a different way. When someone is
grieving the loss of a parent or a partner, nothing can change the
loss. What can change is the way that it is experienced. Perhaps a
change from anger to sadness will enable the patient to begin to
value other relationships again and to begin to treat other people
as worthy to be loved. If this sort of structural change is not possible, there is no justification for taking money for regular and
continuing sessions in long-term therapy.

The question we have to ask is what is it that continues or can
continue and can therefore continue into a changed state? The
best answer that we have come up with so far is to call it 'mind'
and to try to understand what that might mean. Philosophers
and neuro scientists alike have a difficulty with understanding
the human mind. As cosmologists have pointed out, in trying
to explain the Universe, the astronomer has to manage with the
limits of human experience in describing, let alone understanding what is so much larger than human experience. Similarly for
the analytical therapist, the only instrument that we can use to
understand 'mind' is the mind itself.

Repetition as Pattern

From personal experience and from the cosmologists we understand that time moves in one direction only. In the Renaissance, circles and cycles within closed systems formed the predominant patterns of thinking. In the present, we have ceased to think so exclusively in terms of circles and cycles. In the Middle Ages, people were firmly convinced that the Earth was the centre of the Universe and that the solar system could be adequately described if only the circles and ellipses could be made complex enough. They were not inclined to think in terms of an experience happening once and being over and done with. The recurrent rituals of a religion also gave satisfying assurance that patterns could be identified and all could be expected and predicted if one only had enough information in the first place.

Since then, the work of Niclaus Copernicus (1473–1543) and Johannes Kepler (1571–1630) has informed us that the Earth is only a very minor planet that circles round the Sun which is itself a fairly negligible star in one of an infinite number of galaxies. This blow to the narcissism of mankind is an important step on the way to the current limited understanding of the origin of the Universe in the Big Bang and the succession of experiences that were set in motion, all in one direction. Educated people may accept the cosmologists' account of what happened and how we came to be, but looking at the way people function might still lead us to conclude that there is a fondness for repetition and ritual. People, whom we would not describe as obsessional, still have patterns of behaviour that they seek to maintain. We might find these particularly clearly at the edges of the conscious state: getting ready for bed at night, getting up in the morning, for example, seem to be times when people follow patterns that they have set up for themselves and which do not require conscious thought but which are in themselves reassuring in some way.

Rituals are an example of the tendency to want to repeat experiences. The newborn baby is introduced to experience through highly repetitive experiences of feeding, washing, voices, faces and being held in particular ways that do not vary greatly. Thus we are socialised and we continue to seek to repeat. What we consciously like to repeat is, of course, the pleasurable

experience. This sort of repetition can perform a valuable function in holding an individual over time in the sense that repetition links the past with the future. On the other hand, repetition
can be a deadly weight that allows no freedom or creativity. At
its worst it becomes obsessional and stops the individual from
living fully.

Freud was not the first to note and draw attention to this
desire for repetition. Shakespeare's characters are sometimes
bound by their behaviour in the past and the play shows how
they continue to bind themselves. For example, Macbeth, who
has committed two murders, is unable to turn back:

> I am in blood
> Stepped in so far that should I wade no more
> Returning were as tedious as go o'er.   (*Macbeth* III iv)

He has learned the deadly lesson that he is capable of killing and
has found that he is trapped in a repetition of the action that
still is not in any sense pleasurable. He cannot sleep and is tormented with images of blood and bloodshed. For him, repetition
becomes a decline into utter disaster and destruction.

Change, disconnecting from the past is not possible for
Macbeth. He is tormented by the past, particularly by his crimes
and his guilt but the play also shows how aspects of the past
remain effective in determining the present. Macbeth is tormented by guilt over his crime partly because the King whom
he killed had been generous to him. Conflict was started by
his ambitious thoughts and the memory of what he had once
been torments him in his new status of murderer, treacher-
ous host and ungrateful subject. There we already have the
situation of internal tension in which psychodynamic theory
can usefully be applied both to help us to understand what
is causing unhappiness and also to help to relieve the suffering of the individual who, we assume, has developed symptoms
of some sort to help him to ignore the effects of the strife
within him.

The therapist knows that Mr M. (p. 9) came to therapy with
some sort of conflict. At one level the patient knows quite well
what is the matter with him. He has uncontrollable feelings of
rage with his boss and he wants to get rid of them or at least learn

to control them so that he doesn't lose this job and subsequent ones. That is a reasonable agenda. As he has come to a psycho-dynamic therapist he will be invited to consider his present state of mind and to see whether any examination of the past will help him to a better understanding of how he got to be where he is now. If he can allow himself to think about the implication of these patterns he will be free to consider other options. One of the options that he will then have is to consider some sort of cognitive or behaviour therapy to deal with the danger of his anger if he is at that stage unable to control it himself.

Challenging the Patterns of the Profession

At the end of the twentieth and beginning of the twenty-first centuries, Freud's work has been the object of attacks, both for his theory and for the perceived dishonesty of some of his accounts of his cases. An American psychologist speaking to a multidisciplinary gathering of academics at a lecture in Cambridge UK said in 2005 that it was no longer necessary to argue about Freud because his theories are no longer respected by any reputable academics on either side of the Atlantic. By contrast. Drew Westen (1998), a psychologist at Harvard Medical School, agrees that Freud's theories are archaic and obsolete, but argues that Freud's legacy lives on in a number of theoretical propositions that are widely accepted by scientists: the existence of unconscious mental processes; the importance of conflict and ambivalence in behaviour; the childhood origins of adult personality; mental representations as a mediator of social behaviour; and stages of psychological development. These propositions are still of great value to therapists and, in spite of Webster's support, they are all likely to remain subject to lively debate. Freud himself was always ready to modify his theory in the light of new evidence.

Freud's views have had critics on both sides of the Atlantic. The psychologist Frederick Crews (1990) argued that Freud's therapeutic method was to reconstruct childhood experience out of his own imagination and then to implant it in the mind of his patient by suggestion. He also asserted that none of Freud's theories was new enough to merit his fame. Richard

Webster's *Why Freud Was Wrong* (1995) traces Freud's essentially religious personality to his childhood, It shows how the founder of psychoanalysis allowed his messianic dreams to shape the 'science' he created and how, in the diagnostic darkness which prevailed at the beginning of the twentieth century, he led his followers ever deeper into a labyrinth of medical error. Webster questions the basis of Freud's theory of repression because it depends on an asceticism in society or the prevailing culture:

> Psychoanalysis is, I believe, one of the most subtle of our many attempts to use reason in a 'magical' rather than in a scientific manner – to use reason, that is to say, not in order to provide a genuine solution to an intellectual problem, but in order to provide a defence against the forces which we fear, and against aspects of our own nature which arouse anxiety. Freud saw himself as the rational foe of religion. Significantly, however, far from setting out radically to subvert the values of Judaeo-Christian asceticism which were deeply internalised in his own culture, Freud made the Lamarckian assumption that such asceticism had become part of our biological inheritance, so that it now belonged to our very nature. It is for this reason that his notion of therapy contains an implicit endorsement of the oldest of all ascetic ideals – the glorification of the spirit at the expense of the body.   (1995)

Webster was praised by writers such as Anthony Clare and Anthony Storr for this book that had considerable influence. However, as soon as we see from the publisher's blurb that he 'traces' something back to childhood, are we not immediately in the realm that Freud himself created? He is perhaps now so much a part of the cultural milieu in which we grow up that even the psychoanalysts do not always give him the recognition that he deserves for some of his simple truths. Others such as Shakespeare and Nietzsche had known and even made use of some of the same truths as Freud, but no one had expressed these truths in a coherent structure or shown how they could be put together in a therapeutic structure. For this at least, we need to refer to Freud. On the other hand, the critique that accuses him and his followers of using suggestion to an extreme or unwarranted extent is a serious criticism and needs to be carefully examined by each practitioner.

Other critics have focussed on Freud's personal shortcomings. Richard Webster's systematic analysis of Freud presents an image of a man driven by ambition. Freud's well known disputes with his colleagues such as Carl Jung and Ernest Jones have also shown us a man who was proud and impatient of criticism. These points may be valid but do not prevent us from recognising that he has made accessible to us ideas that are still useful and creative in the therapeutic context. Debates accompanied the progress of Freud's ideas in Europe and are still continuing.

Meanwhile, in America, Freud gained an even wider following both among writers and scholars, not just among those who would become psychoanalysts. After reading some of Freud's work the novelist Theodore Dreiser wrote in the following terms of his achievement:

> Every paragraph came as a revelation to me – a strong revealing light thrown on some of the darkest problems that haunted and troubled me and my work. And reading him has helped me in my studies of life and men...[H]e reminded me of a conqueror who has taken a city, entered its age-old, hoary prisons and there generously proceeded to release from their gloomy and rusted cells the prisoners of formulae, faiths and illusions which have racked and worn man for hundreds and thousands of years...The light that he has thrown on the human mind! Its vagaries and destructive delusions and their cure! It is to me at once colossal and beautiful! (1982)

The whole climate of opinion that Auden ascribed to Freud's work has been appropriately challenged for all sorts of reasons but few have denied the relevance of the concept of the unconscious. In the United States, Richard Kihlstrom argues not that transference does not happen but he does question whether or not it has therapeutic effects:

> No empirical evidence indicates [that] the mechanisms by which psychoanalysis achieves its effects, such as they are, are those specifically predicated on the theory such as transference and catharsis. (Kihlstrom 2003: 9)

This leaves many questions still unanswered but nothing that has been said so far detracts from the pragmatic value of applying the concept of patterns of behaviour to helping people to understand what is holding them in counter productive behaviour and thinking. Of course Freud set ideas in motion that challenge our view of ourselves as subjects in control of our own minds. Not surprisingly he encountered much hostility for this alone. Debate is a sign of life and vigour and the heat of argument can allow new forms to emerge. We can appreciate the need to reassess and reappraise what we do and why we do it even while saying that the framework is still useful. This book will therefore work on the assumption that patterns formed in the past are important in forming the present mental environment of any individual.

What is Transference?

Transference is a mental process by which the human mind makes what is lost and gone still present in the people and things that are available to be seen and heard.

The British psychoanalyst Charles Rycroft, in his *Critical Dictionary of Psychoanalysis* (1968), worked from the assumption that Freud's ideas were worth assembling and that his terminology was worth defining. He defined transference in a two-page article, which begins with the statement that it is a

> process by which a patient displaces onto his analyst feelings, ideas, etc, which derive from previous figures in his life... (1968: 168)

These figures that are no longer present are preserved through the transferring of patterns of reaction. This is often counterproductive in that the relationships that we project onto the present are often destructive and damaging. Perhaps the purpose in doing so is to reproduce the bad past in the hope that somehow it can be made better. There is much more to be said about what can be transferred and the conditions in which transference operates. This book will explore both the process and the content of transference in greater depth.

Projection is the Process

To begin with the mechanism: since transference is a process of projection, what is a projection and how does it work? Can a projection be changed or removed?

Anyone who tries to understand the working of the human mind has to use a human mind to do it. We cannot be objective. We can look only through the lens of our own perceptions. Perceptions are not objective but are processed by each individual before they come to awareness. When I look at a tree, I will see on some days, a beautiful and mysterious aspect of creation. I might think philosophical thoughts about it. How does it know how to grow so that it makes the particular shape of its species? Why does it not go on growing taller for the whole of its life? On another day I might envy the tree because it can stand apparently undisturbed by human problems. Yet again I see the tree as gnarled and old and weary, bowing down under the weight of its leaves and its years. Each of these perceptions is partly to do with the tree itself, but much more to do with my own state of mind. I *project* my fears of old age onto the tree and then see them embodied in the inanimate object in front of me. I then react to what I think I see. Strictly speaking, projection is happening when I see an image of my own in the person or thing in front of me. I react as though the feelings did indeed belong to the other.

Freud described the possibility of projection when he tried to understand the problems of his paranoid patient Dr Schreber. In 1911, Freud set out his understanding that the man who so feared his own homosexual attraction to another man that he assumed the unconscious proposition for himself: 'I do not love him, I hate him because HE PERSECUTES ME.' The projection of feelings of hatred contained a defence against Schreber's own feelings of love and a rationale for the defensive hatred.

Freud hypothesised that the paranoid delusions that the man he loved actually hated and persecuted Schreber were created unconsciously because they were needed for protection against unacceptable feelings (1911: 201). This interpretation of Schreber's delusions has been challenged by, for example, Paul Zeal (2006: 460) who sees the problem for Schreber as the universal difficulty of accommodating femininity. That is not the same thing as homosexuality. Whatever the accuracy of Freud's view of Schreber's delusions, the idea of projection as a form of defence has been of great use in understanding inexplicably strong feelings.

Jung's View of Transference

Carl Jung, on the other hand had relatively little to say directly. He contributed to our thinking a metaphor which has been endlessly generative. The *Critical Dictionary of Jungian Analysis* (Samuels: 1986) has no entry on transference but refers the reader to some other articles, such as that on *Alchemy*. Those who might call themselves *Jungians* vary in the amount of importance that they attach to the concept of transference itself but they do attach great importance to the processes of change and the process by which projections can be withdrawn.

Carl Jung based his ideas about change on processes that he had discovered through his intellectual explorations of the cultural history of man. He was of course also aware of Freud's ideas and was in some measure reacting to them. He chose the imagery derived from the study of alchemy to express his own views. Alchemy is a particularly suitable set of metaphors because the whole aim of the alchemists was to bring about change. They set about changing base metals to something more valuable such as gold and tried to transform matter into immortal spirit. The alchemical processes for enabling this change were well known and because they are all about the actual process of change, they were particularly suitable for trying to say something about how we might imagine trying to change the set patterns of the mind which can seem as hard as a solid mineral.

In the sixteenth and seventeenth centuries, the process of alchemical change had become very complex and was documented in various texts. The alchemist worked by bringing together opposites and he (the usually male alchemist) needed a female assistant who might be real or symbolic. The elements to be changed were contained in a vessel known as the *vas*. Immediately, we have a description of the therapeutic situation in which the alchemist or therapist and the assistant (patient) must play their different, often opposing roles within the confines of the therapeutic hour. Very often the process involved heating the elements in the *vas* and we know very well that there is usually an intensification of emotions within the early stages of therapy simply because of the confinement within the setting both in terms of time and its limitations and in terms of the place which must be safely enclosed and protected from the outside world but is therefore frightening because of the intensity that it generates.

Jung then described various stages of the alchemical process, of which one of the best known is the *nigredo* or *blackening*. This was thought to be the point at which the alchemist could see that some major change was about to take place. In terms of the metals, it was the point at which the two elements were melted down and mingled. No longer in their original state, they might combine to form new materials or to give off spirit. In terms of the transference, there is a sense in which this represents the first stage of what must happen. The two people in the relationship react to each other in various ways and in the heated and unusual context of the *vas* a certain melting down of the original form of each may take place. What this image unfortunately does not show so clearly is that there are two kinds of joining together that can go on inside the *vas*. One is the relationship of the patient to the therapist in which the patient seeks to change and to find different resolutions to problems. The other is the illusional relationship in which the patient projects his own past experience onto the therapist and the therapist in turn projects onto him. Both of these relationships will experience some degree of melt down and re-forming in the therapeutic process.

Jung was working in the knowledge of the discoveries that Freud had already made. Freud was very preoccupied with the question of change and how it might be encouraged. In 1912 he had concluded that the amount of change possible was very limited when he had restricted himself to working with hypnosis. Like the therapists who have followed him, Freud knew that hypnosis can be very helpful but its effects were limited and did not usually bring about fundamental changes in mental structures. He concluded that this was because of the resistance to the therapeutic process that all therapists encounter and try to understand. His answer to this difficulty was a fundamental idea about the therapeutic relationship. The patient comes to see his therapist saying that he wants to change but in fact this is only part of the truth. There is internal conflict which is fought between the wish to change and get better, and the wish to remain safely hidden within the confines of the symptoms which are the defences against full recognition of his truth (see Chapter 4).

Freud's important conclusion was that the resistances must be understood. They are there for a reason. If we do not understand the reason for the resistance, then we might as well be King Canute trying to hold back the tide as tell the patient that he needs to change his behaviour for his own sake.

In order to work out the reasons for this particular person to resist his own truth, Freud asserted the importance of allowing the patient to develop his transference to the analyst. That means that in the therapeutic situation, the transference is both the enemy of change and its greatest help. When love is denied or is not sufficient for a person to live by, the feelings have been hidden away but have not disappeared. In the powerful and intimate atmosphere of the therapy, these feelings that were usually first encountered in childhood are rediscovered.

This happens at first without any conscious awareness on the part of the patient. Freud points out that the only way one can know that it is happening is when the flow of free association stops. He says that he then points out that there is something to do with the person of the analyst and the patient is holding back from saying what it is. Freud's paradigm implies that when the analyst points out this reason for silence or deflection, the patient invariably is able to move on. We might modify this technique somewhat in order to lessen the authoritarian, suggestiveness of the therapist, but silence usually does have something to do with the anxiety of the speaker in front of the listener. The connection may be a matter of shame or a matter of hostility but in most cases, the failure or refusal to speak can be traced to a connection with the fact that speaking takes place in the context of speaking to someone from the past or in front of someone from the past whose presence was of emotional and strategic importance.

Mrs C entered the room of a therapist whom she had agreed to consult. She looked around the room that she was entering for the second time and said: 'this is not as comfortable as

I expected it to be. I don't like the colours that you've got in here. I thought therapists usually had soothing colours but this is not very restful. It's too dark as well'. The therapist remained in a waiting mode expecting that she would find out who was the person whose room was uncomfortable. It was too soon to raise it in a challenging way, but she did say 'I get the impression that you have been in a room that was uncomfortable in this way before.'

Mrs C was not willing to respond to that but several sessions later, she said 'you were right about that. My grandmother's room was a bit like this. I used to get sent to sit with her and I knew that my mother sent me there when she was going to see her boyfriend.'

The therapist was very interested in this connection because it made sense of the hostility as well as the anxiety about whether something else was going on. Both patient and therapist were concerned that something was happening somewhere else and that continued as a theme of the therapy.

If Therapy is Worth Doing, it's Worth Resisting

The next major development in the theory of transference was made by Anna Freud and Melanie Klein. Anna Freud developed her father's ideas about defences in a detailed discussion of the way in which the ego is involved in the process of defence and resistance to the therapy. She points out that the transference of the relationship that the infant or child experienced into the adult situation can lead to 'acting in the transference'. In other words, the therapist may hear of behaviour outside the therapy that seems to relate to the infantile relationship that has been activated in the therapy. This is an area where our responsibilities are great and we shall discuss this further in Chapter 6. Gross behaviour such as promiscuity or self harm outside the therapy is usually also traceable to a response to a figure from the past. It may be a punishment to someone or it may be an echo of someone's behaviour. In either case, the past will reveal the origin of the current pattern.

Acting out defensive behaviour in the patient's present life can be a very difficult problem for therapists. The intention of course is that it should be difficult and that in itself has a transferential implication. Defining and identifying this sort of defence is problematic and fraught with danger. Some analytic therapists would consider the formation of any external loving relationship during therapy as a defence against the strength of the positive transference: 'I do not love you, I love him or her'. Others would count the formation of such a relationship as a sign that they have successfully helped the patient out of their neurotic isolation. The reasonable position must take account of both possibilities without leaping to conclusions and making statements from the therapist's position of authority along he lines of 'he or she is not right for you'.

Negative acting out is perhaps clearer. The patient who attacks the authority figure at work may be causing himself a great deal of trouble as a result of not being able to attack the therapist and see that one person can be both good and bad. The parent is not intended to be able to deal with the behaviour to his or her own satisfaction. In so far as the therapist begins to stand for the parent then she will receive feelings and behaviour intended for the parent. Why should the patient allow satisfaction to the parent whom he blames for so much? The anxiety or reactive anger of the therapist who is being tested by the patient will be part of the scenario which the patient needs to recreate and the therapist is trusted to find a way to confront it that is constructive, just as the parent of an adolescent needs to find the way to exert enough authority to maintain discipline while still remembering what it was like to be sixteen or eighteen years old.

In popular accounts of therapy we read such statements as 'It was not just transference. I really did love him'. This indicates a popular misconception that transference refers only to some sort of false or non-genuine love. This concept of transference is a travesty of what it means. All love from the most passing fancy to the life long love of committed partners has transference in it according to the definition that I am using. Patterns from the past enable us to learn and to function. Without them we would have to learn everything over again each time we meet someone. We can usefully transfer the trust and warmth of early experiences that were good. Transference is only a problematic error if it is from such a narcissistic point of view that the presence of the person now has no effect on the nature of the reaction and therefore it cannot be corrected or modified. Escaping from the power of the pattern means acquiring the ability to see a little more clearly the person who is actually with me now.

The concentrated atmosphere of the consulting room facilitates production of the patient's patterns both harmful and benevolent. The therapist must have the wisdom and the patient must have the courage to accept what is happening and to think about it. The patient will not be able to think about what is happening to him at first but if the therapy is useful, he will gradually learn to catch hold of his own negative and damaging patterns and change them into something that is appropriate to the present. He will keep and develop his ability to love and will take his love to another person outside of the therapy. The difficulties engendered in that process will be addressed in Chapter 5.

Conclusion

This chapter has examined the universal nature of transference patterns. They appear in every aspect of human relationship, both those we have with other people and those within ourselves. Since we can expect to come across the operation of patterns from the past in human encounters, we might expect to find these patterns in the therapist's approach to the patient. Therapists practising analytic therapy are required to have their own analytic therapy so that they have some chance of being able to identify and reflect on their own experience in a session. This does not make the task an easy one. The next chapter will look at some of the difficulties facing the therapist who tries to find ways of making her own experience a help rather than a hindrance in the therapeutic process.

Discussion Points

1. Jane is a woman of 46 who comes to see a therapist because she has a conflicted relationship with her daughter. She says that they argue over small things

(Continued)

and her daughter criticizes the way she looks:, e.g. 'you can't go out in that Mum'. The therapist finds that she has suffered from a critical and demanding mother who never appreciated her.

a.   Should the therapist say anything about possible implications for the therapeutic relationship in the assessment session and if so, what?

2.   What use can you make in your work of your understanding of the meaning of *the unconscious*?
3.   What do you mean by *mind*?
4.   What do you think of the evidence for saying that the past affects the presence?

2 Transference and its Mirror Image: Counter-transference

Questions to consider while reading

1. What is *counter-transference*?
2. Can the term be used to excuse poor practice?
3. What are the dangers of paying attention to counter-transference?
4. What has Lacan contributed to our thinking on transference and the role of the analyst?

Introduction

Chapter 1 examined the prevalence of pattern in human mental processes and in our emotional life. It looked also at the effect of experience in setting up patterns that can then become traps to hold each subject in a repetition which is painful and counter productive. This chapter will begin to address the ways in which the therapist who is also inevitably affected by her own patterns can use her experience in the therapeutic relationship to help in her understanding of the process. The analytic therapist benefitting from the discoveries of Freud, Klein and Jung has the potential to make the problems and difficulties of repetition into the tools for constructing new, more satisfactory patterns. The involvement of the therapist makes her into the participant observer who has to maintain two roles and be open to the full impact of the emotions generated in the session and also to step back and think about them. She particularly needs to scrutinise her interventions to consider whether they are emerging from her transference to the patient without being processed. This need

29

for the ability to be doing two things at once is one of the reasons for the long and demanding training required of analytic therapists.

If you search for the word *transference* in the papers that have been written in professional journals in English in the 1990's and the start of the twenty first century, you will find that the majority of articles are actually on the subject of *counter-transference*. The greatest developments in theory have come in the area of the therapist's understanding of his or her own reaction to the patient. By 1912, Freud had understood the value of the appearance of the emotions that could not be explained by the 'real' actions and character of the therapist. These emotional manifestations could be understood only as the appearances of some past, mostly buried remnants of earlier experiences. To begin with they had been seen as a problem. They were the psychiatric equivalent of the fat that gets in the way of the surgeon trying to operate on a deeply embedded tumour. By 1912, however, Freud had understood that these very emotions, because they were inappropriate, could be seen as a re-enactment of early scenarios. The re-enactment gave the physician the opportunity to play a part in the patient's mental life and through this to make changes to mental patterns.

Transference to the Patient or Counter-transference?

By the time of the death of Freud in 1939, the idea that experiences could be transferred from the distant past onto a person in the present by the process of projection had been set out clearly. This theoretical concept implied that the therapist would interpret the patient's material as telling something about the patient whatever its surface content appeared to be. Sometimes patients complain about the therapist being lazy or useless or abusing him in various ways. But sometimes the therapist really was abusing him in some way, or was being neglectful or seductive. The theory required that the therapist should put as little of herself as possible into the mix. However hard the therapist tries to remain neutral, keeping her own experiences in the background, the clinical situation will include the therapist's transference to the patient as well as the patient's transference to the therapist. If the therapist manages to remain receptive enough to experience the full force of the patient's transference, she will have her own response to it. There are several narratives that we can tell about what happens and perhaps no absolute truth. Anyone who has experience of dealing with patients' complaints will be well aware that we can have two completely different accounts of what happened both in terms of the emotional tone and also in terms of the supposed facts themselves.

Counter-transference Becomes a Useful Tool

In the 1950s Paula Heimann initiated the theory of counter-transference. This new approach enabled the therapist to think about her contribution in a focussed and eventually a useful way.

Paula Heimann published her seminal paper on the counter-transference in 1950 and showed that not only the patient's emotional response to the events of the therapy, but also that of the therapist could be useful in understanding the emotional life of the patient. She acknowledges that there was confusion over the meaning of the term. As with *transference* itself she noted the tendency to use the word to refer to any feelings that were present in the relationship. Alternatively, it can be restricted to the therapist's transference to the patient.

Our basic assumption is that the therapist's unconscious understands that of his patient. This rapport on the deep level comes to the surface in the form of feelings which the analyst notices in response to his patient as his 'counter-transference' (1950: 82).

Heimann was stating the idea that the understanding that the therapist can offer to the patient arises at least in part from the process of transference. The patient is able to communicate at an unconscious level to the therapist who is trained to reflect and interpret rather than to react to the feelings engendered in her by the patient.

The counter-transference is not just a matter of the therapist's transference to the patient.

> ## Possible definitions of counter-transference:
>
> 1. The therapist's immediate emotional response to the patient
> 2. All the feelings which the therapist experiences towards his patient
> 3. The therapist's transference to his patient which is therefore unconscious.

All three possible definitions have been and still are in use, but the first two are so inclusive that they are not very useful. If the third definition, the therapist's response to the patient's transference, is taken as the most useful definition, it becomes essential for the therapist both to bring into consciousness, consider and to articulate what is being transferred from the past into the therapeutic relationship and what her own reaction to that has been. Heimann argues that the purpose of a training therapy is partly to help the therapist to use this valuable but delicate tool with some degree of accuracy. If we are to accept Heimann's contention that the therapist's experience is the 'patient's creation' (1950: 83), there is clearly considerable danger that the therapist will confuse what she brings to the situation with what the patient is communicating. This is a danger which can never be completely avoided but against which the therapist must do her best to be on guard. Heimann had perhaps more faith in the value of therapy to enable the therapist herself to understand her own infantile conflicts than is entirely warranted. Those who intend to try to work with interpretations derived from an understanding of counter-transference are required by technical considerations but more importantly by ethical concerns to have a training therapy in which the training therapist models the use of this kind of understanding of what happens in therapy.

The Dangers of Counter-transference

At the point when counter-transference was brought to the forefront in the 1950s, Freud had already written about the need to work with resistance in order to undo repression. The whole of psychoanalytic method was already based on the task of unravelling the strands of the feelings through which the parental figures would be projected onto the therapist to enable the patient to relive the conflicts that were still harassing him in adulthood. Heimann's ideas about the different aspects of countertransference helped to refine the instrument that the therapist could use to understand why patients always seem to resist and why they refuse to allow the ideas that cause suffering cannot be allowed to become conscious.

One interesting statement made by Heimann is that emotions can be recognised as counter-transference by the way they are experienced by the therapist. When the material and the interpretations are getting close to something that has been repressed to protect the patient from an unwelcome emotion or recognition, the therapist will experience a force with energy behind it rather than just lethargy. Even lethargy in the therapist will need to be examined as a counter-transference response which may indicate the enchanted sleep that is imposed on the characters in a fairy tale to prevent the knight from rescuing the princess from the evil enchanter. Many 'other defence mechanisms will arouse other qualities in the therapist's response' (1950: 64).

In the conclusion to her paper, Heimann refers to the 'problem of counter-transference'. She was working with the early view that counter-transference was, like transference itself, a problem to be overcome. Freud had seen the therapist's own feelings as a hindrance to understanding the feelings of the patient as I said earlier. No-one has suggested that they are not sometimes a problem and are certainly a problem if the therapist reacts rather than thinking about what she feels. More recently, these responses have been seen to have positive use. For example, the person-centred school of psychotherapy is less concerned to distinguish between the different origins of emotional responses but would seek to use the therapist's response to achieve *congruence* with the patient. Achieving congruence means expressing honestly what the therapist is feeling in response to the patient. This obviously does also guarantee that the feelings *are* in response to the patient and not merely engendered by something that the therapist is currently going though in her own external life.

Checking with the patient will usually establish whether the feel-, ing has anything to do with him or is just engendered by the therapist.

A therapist may be experiencing any of a myriad of emotions while listening to a patient. Heimann gives us an example of a patient whom she had 'taken over from a colleague':

> The patient was a man in his forties who had originally sought treatment when his marriage broke down. Among his symptoms promiscuity figured prominently. In the third week of his analysis with me he told me at the beginning of the session that he was going to marry a woman whom he had met only a short time before.

On hearing such a statement at the beginning of a session, most therapists would be paying conscious attention and would be processing the information as well as their own response to it. What is likely is that the therapist would be experiencing some sort of emotional response and we could not tell what that might be without knowing a great deal more about the preceding session and the way in which the news was delivered. Heimann tells us that she felt 'a sense of apprehension and worry'. Trainee therapists might well worry that they have heard that Freud advised patients not to make life changing decisions while in therapy so what will the supervisor say? On the other hand, what right does a therapist have to tell a patient what he should or should not do? In other words, a state of conflict is likely.

In this case, the patient went on to tell his therapist his dream about wanting to repair a second hand car that he had bought. Someone was objecting and telling him that he should be cautious.

This caused confusion. The therapist herself felt worried that she was missing something even more serious than the wish to sabotage the analysis by having a more important emotional relationship outside. She listened to this feeling and it was reinforced by the patient who said that he thought the second hand car stood for the therapist and that he wanted to repair her but was being hindered by the voice of reason and caution which said that maybe he should not get so involved. In the analytic view, the therapist might often be considered as standing for the parent in symbolic terms and this patient in these terms was conveying the complexity of his feelings about his mother.

A less experienced therapist might have plunged into interpreting the desire for another woman as a wish to evade the intensity of the analytic situation and would have missed something very important in doing so.

Therapists usually have an emotional response to a new patient. This can be informative; it can also act as a warning.

> Ms T came to see a counsellor. She said that her problem was that she binged on food and then vomited. She had been to see a number of counsellors and none of them had been able to help her. She had a very difficult relationship with a partner who was saying that he wanted a separation. She was noted to be tall but not overweight. She said however, that she was not happy with the way she looked and thought that she needed to change her appearance so that her partner would not leave her.

The counsellor reported that she had thought that the bulimia was not too severe and she would be happy to work with her. She added 'about a day after I saw her I became very anxious about seeing her and I realise that I am quite frightened of her.' In supervision a decision was taken that she needed specialist help and that the counsellor would not work with her. She told Ms T that her interests would be best served by going to a specialist in eating problems and the route to this would be via the physician. The patient was extremely angry on being told this and threatened to make a complaint that she felt the counsellor was incompetent.

There was much to be learned from this experience with Ms T. On the one hand, people need plenty of warning that an *assessment* is just that and both parties must be free to decide whether continuing with the therapy will be in the best interests of the patient. It also demonstrates that the therapist's fear could be seen as a warning because it might have indicated that the patient was herself afraid and was not ready to enter into the intimate space of the therapeutic relationship. Perhaps we should conclude that the patient/therapist pair in this example was not likely to work well together. Why not? Surely the therapist should be able to overcome her own feelings? This is a difficult question to answer. Such inferences must always be treated with great caution and be acted upon only with the proviso that one might well be wrong. In matters of a relationship as crucial as the therapeutic one, the therapist might be better to err on the side of caution. Both therapist and patient will come with some pre-formed transference to the beginning of therapy.

Pre-formed Transference

A patient comes to a therapist with all sorts of ideas about what therapy means for him or her. These ideas may have come directly from the person who makes the referral. These may be the ideas that therapy can actually help and the therapist will be professional, kind, authoritative or something else in the realm of the positive. From the social and cultural environment some negative ideas will also affect most people. These ideas may be derived from the media. Woody Allen's films have depicted the American fashion for the talking therapies. He depicts analysis as comic and as one of the accoutrements of middle class angst but not as leading anywhere constructive. Allen's whole comic universe depends on the belief that things do not change fundamentally. Depression is the appropriate mood because that reveals the universe is a sad place in which we exhibit our pathetic pretensions and our hopes and fears seem ridiculously grandiose.

There are many other media images of analysis and psychotherapy in Europe and the Americas. From all sorts of enthusiastic praise and critique in the mass media, each individual will have some hopes reinforced and some fears given shape. In addition to or against the force of the cultural background, will come the transference of each individual to the therapist's voice on the telephone or answerphone in giving the original message. The therapist may answer questions at this stage or may prevaricate and seek to give all information and explanations at the first face-to-face meeting. If the patient experiences this first encounter as withholding, the transference that will already be taking shape at the first meeting is from an early figure who withheld gratification from the infant. This is not necessarily a problem. We have all had the experience of being denied gratification and we all have developed ways of managing the waiting or the frustration.

The patient will perhaps show the response to the frustration very early in the first meeting and that in itself may be a serious problem for the therapist. The therapist who met Ms T might have been experiencing her defence against the fear that she would not be satisfied or helped. The fear that this would happen might have been expelled from the mind of the patient and unconsciously transferred to the mind of the therapist. That may be the case as the patient seems to have experienced something close to annihilation in the past which has left her highly sensitive and unable to deal with frustration.

The therapist's pre-formed transference will come from the complex network of training and therapeutic experience of her own. She will have been affected by the cultural and social milieu but the negative messages of the media will be relegated to the background. She will have to make an effort to put herself back in the place of the patient who might be new to therapy and might not know what to expect. If the patient is already experienced in therapy, there will be some sort of emotion transferred from whatever kind of experience that might have been. For that reason alone, it is important to ask about the experience of previous therapy at some point in the first few meetings, giving the therapist some idea of the kind of figure of a therapist that might have already fused with the father or mother.

When all these aspects of pre-formed transference have been considered, the therapist may be left with her own powerful and unique response to this patient. The therapist meeting Ms T was left with her fear. Should she have overcome it? The subsequent events seemed to indicate that the patient did not actually wish to submit herself to the long hard work of analysis, much less of becoming a patient who submits herself in some ways to the power and authority of the therapist. The fear that the therapist experiences can sometimes be an indication that the patient has a psychotic area or is even a full-blown psychotic or psychopath. For this reason also, the therapist must pay attention to the quality of her fear and must decide whether it is the normal anxiety about beginning work with a new person or whether it is something much more intense and inexplicable. This kind of fear tends to be described in emotional terms such as 'an icy fear' or.

'cold fear'. In any case, the feeling bears no relation to anything that the patient has actually said or done.

Transference has therefore a role in the initial decision making about the process of therapy that could and should be undertaken. As transference will inevitably appear in the first session it will enable the therapist to judge the nature of the problems that the person is bringing and also will enable her to decide whether she is willing and able to work with the kind of transference that is initially developing. Some forms of hysteria and narcissism will lead to fits of violent rage and an attempt to control the other person. These may not appear in their pure form but they will give rise to some sort of reaction in the therapist. This is helpful because inexperienced therapists and those who are tired or not working at their best for some reason, should probably not take on such a person.

The existence of this sort of transference might also warn the therapist of Ms T that she will have to be very careful in saying that she does not intend to offer ongoing therapy. In this case, an extra assessment session was offered but was rejected. The therapist must expect an angry response to rejection. How she deals with this is an ongoing and difficult question which cannot be easily answered. Each therapist is well advised to consider how best to speak honestly and openly to the patient about the reasons for thinking that someone else might be more helpful.

The French Critique of Transference

Not everyone would agree that transference can be used in a straightforward way or that counter-transference can be used in a way that is helpful. In the first half of the twentieth century, Jacques Lacan urged a return to Freud but at the same time was advocating a thorough overhaul of Freudian theory and its conclusions. His ideas were not acceptable to the psychoanalytic establishment which expelled Lacan from the International Psychoanalytic Association in 1963. He then formed his École Freudienne in 1964. When his own theory was in danger of being understood and acquiring an orthodoxy of its own, he dissolved his school and founded La Cause Freudienne. In spite of

or perhaps because of his status as arch rebel, Lacan has continued to influence psychoanalysis throughout the world, not only
in France or the rest of Europe. The ideas of Lacan should not be
ignored because they are often difficult to grasp and sometimes
revolutionary. They facilitate careful thinking about the reasons
for holding to or modifying existing beliefs. Challenges can be
destructive but they can also be used to make thinking clearer
and to delineate a position.

In the 1950's Jacques Lacan was pursuing a fundamentalist
purity of his own and in some ways he was closer to Jung than
to Freud in his view of the transference. He shared Jung's interest
in the elaboration of dreams. He was, however, totally committed to the concept of the unconscious and its implications for
theory and clinical practice. He was also interested in the person
of the analyst and the way in which he figures in the material
of the patient. He emphasised that the analyst who shows some
understanding of the patient's ideas and feelings and above all
of his dreams, begins to be felt by the patient to be the *cause* of
these phenomena from the unconscious. This effect is increased
if the analyst manages to achieve the kind of interpretations that
Lacan advocates. Following Freud he argues that the purpose of
analysis is to reveal the unconscious desire, to track it down and
to own it. To help to achieve this, the analyst must listen to what
is not said as much as to what is said. She must listen for the
gaps, the hesitations, the places where the subject is changed. If
she does so, she then must frame interpretations that are equivo-
cal. Only an interpretation which puzzles and confuses the ego is
likely to get behind the resistance and enable the 'beauty behind
the shutter' to be glimpsed.

Of course, the therapist who is able to utter enigmatic
pronouncements, which on reflection provide some jewel of
meaning, will become an oracular figure, speaking in some
degree for the unconscious. She will be established as Cause.
Lacan gives the word a capital letter to emphasise that there is a
power in the emotion felt by the patient who is going though this
stage. His therapist becomes the one who is supposed to know
everything and has all the answers if only she would tell him
what they are. From this point the therapist takes the place of
the parent who held the power of life and death over the young
child and becomes the locus of oedipal longing for the love of the

parent. Bernard Burgoyne points out that Lacan in his analytic work pursued a kind of Socratic dialogue so that:

> The Socratic dialogue evokes the oedipal love relationships that remain otherwise repressed and this brings into being the production of the transference... broken or interrupted tasks are remembered much more significantly than assignations that have been allowed to run towards their end... Lacan's introduction of the variable length of session is in part based on the same principle: both Socratic dialogue and the variable session evoke the love relations of childhood. (1997: 50)

This is a point of technique where we certainly cannot all agree. The variable session is notorious and much caricatured. The therapist who has been trained to regard the prompt beginning and end of the fifty minute hour as a part of the reliability which she offers to the patient and which enables him to take risks with his own feelings and memories may think it extraordinary that a Lacanian would decide that there is a point of emotional intensity at which the session could be most fruitfully ended. On the other hand, it does represent the shock tactics that can be seen as a form of trial of the view that the end justifies the means. The bewildered and indignant patient, thrown out of his session after five minutes will certainly think hard about what made his therapist decide to end the session at that moment. His attachment to her will no doubt lead to a process that is both conscious and unconscious about the meaning of the short session. Philip Hill (2003) quotes a colleague whose sessions were regularly ended after a few minutes. He was able eventually to understand that the therapist was telling him that his dryly intellectual material was a waste of time (2003: xx).

Lacan's major contribution was to emphasise that human beings do not use language. Language uses us. The community and society in which we live already has language and we arrive in a structure that already exists so that it shapes our thinking. The unconscious, Lacan famously said, is structured like a language though not the language of conscious thought. In fact it is language. Our wishes, thoughts, dreams come to the conscious mind in words if at all. Slips of the tongue or perfectly deliberate statements hold within them the threads that lead us back to the unconscious origins of conscious thought if only we grasp the end of the thread. Lacan also returned to Freud's work on the wish in order to elaborate the importance of Desire. Few concepts are more important in the analysis of patterns than desire. There is often the question in therapeutic work 'what does this person want?'. Most particularly in time limited work the patient and therapist together need to find a focus which usually encapsulates the desire of the patient for a change in him or herself. When the patient is alienated from desire it is very difficult to ensure that the desire is that of the patient and not that of the therapist alone.

Lacan's thinking helps us to analyse whose desire is being expressed. The traditional approach to transference would locate this question in terms of compliance. Whose desire is the patient seeking to satisfy? Does he want to satisfy his mother's desire? Or his father's? We can see that for some of the time the patient is likely to seek to please the therapist in the way that the child might seek to please a parent. In the transference, the mother's desire has been internalised to the extent that the patient does not know what his own desire might be. There is much more to say about desire. One of the points most relevant to transference is the distinction between demand and desire. Demand is something that therapists often have to hear:

> Change my time
> Charge me less
> Don't go away
> Don't end the session
> Don't see other people
> Think about me all the time

Why is Language so Important in Transference?

The small baby has no language but from before birth has been familiar with the sound of his mother's voice. He hears her more clearly after birth and gradually begins to understand tones of voice, separating the loving gentle voice of the relaxed feeding mother from the anxious, tense or angry voice of the mother who has no milk or no time. Desire in the infant begins to depend in his mind on his mother's desire. She is the powerful one who can make everything all right for him or not. Here begins a process of development in which the desire of the (m)other is more important than anything. The infant's 'wise needs' as Bice Benvenuto (1986) calls them, can safely translate into desire only if the mother's desire can be satisfied. This is a highly problematic experience. How does the young infant know how to satisfy the mother's desire? Nature gives the small baby the ability to smile and this seems to help greatly in the early bonding process. After that, he is on his own to figure it out.

With this unsatisfied longing in the background, the therapeutic experience is a re-creation of the situation in which the mother must be pleased by the infant who does not know how to satisfy her and does not in any case have the power to do so. That explains in some measure why the patterns that return in the therapeutic relationship are so strongly emotional and often erotic as the patient tries to make himself sufficient for his therapist in the way that he might have wanted once to be sufficient for his mother. Through the transference that appears in analytic work, the therapist can help the patient to find the words for the knowledge that has been too dangerous to know. At this point, Lacan's developmental story brings us to the mirror. In his essay written in 1949 'The mirror stage as formative of the function of the I', he describes how the small infant sees himself held up in an adult's arms and smiles with great pleasure at the image in the glass. He thinks, says Lacan (1977), that he is beautiful, strong and whole. This is a misconception and it lies at the heart of all adult thinking. It is the beginning of narcissism and the beginning of the misperception of the ego which continues as self deception throughout life. We shall return to this problem in Chapter 5. For the moment, the main conclusion to be drawn from Lacan's ideas is as Ellie Ragland put it:

> The analyst's goal is to trip up the orderly gait of the patient's recited memories, conscious fantasies . . . self descriptions . . . in order to push him askew of his assumed way of seeing himself. (1995: 126)

This is a difficult task and there is an ethical responsibility to pushing someone 'askew' which is why the task can be undertaken fully only after a thorough consideration of the patient's readiness.

Transference of Desire, Demand and Need

Lacan makes a useful distinction between the *desire*, the *demand* and the *need*. Each of these will appear in the transference of the earlier situation to the present and will need different treatment by the therapist. Part of the therapist's task is to distinguish between these three and to help the patient to recognise his desire as distinct from his demand. Demand is conceptualised by Lacan to be the repeated request for something to be given and its purpose is to discover what it is that will not be given or cannot be given. Perhaps that can be desired. Need of course is based on the bodily requirements of the infant for food, protection and shelter. When these three have been recognised and separated, the patient will be able to recognise his needs. The therapist using these ideas therefore is looking at her experience of the patient and weighing the demands that he makes. The demands will not be met so that as a result, the patient must despair of satisfaction and begin to discover what is the purpose of the demands. The patient for example who consistently asks 'what should I do?' is making a demand which he partly knows the therapist will not fulfil but he keeps asking because his purpose is to prove to himself that love is not enough. He may love his therapist but that will not compel her to answer him. He will eventually come to the realisation that the only thing he can count on is himself and his own desire.

Why is his own desire so important? Is this emphasis not going to lead to the creation of a tribe of immensely selfish monsters? Some practitioners of the 'let it all hang out' schools of thought might well be encouraging people to throw aside the limits imposed by the superego. Freud and those who have followed him are not in any way joining with this alliance. Freud was interested in the ways in which the ego could control the engines of desire. Lacan places no trust in the ability of the ego to do anything but deceive in the interests of a more comfortable self image. One of his central beliefs, following Freud is that people generally deceive themselves and do not wish to know the truth. Nevertheless, both would agree that recognition of the desire of the individual as distinct from the desires that have come from another is vital in order to reduce self deception and to help people to live closer to reality. In this process transference is a therapeutic tool of precision and power.

Who is Speaking to Whom?

Lacan's view that the mind deceives itself is shared by all analytic theorists. It gives a whole different complexion to the therapeutic encounter. We find that we do not know at the beginning of any session, never mind the beginning of therapy, who is talking to whom? This is one of the most relevant and useful questions to ask. Many therapists have an inkling of this question and will ask it in relation to the superego. When a cruel voice is detected, speaking in the first person, the therapist may well ask 'whose voice is that?' Asking this question all the time is our task. In the terms of the language theorists, we are asking about the way in which the subject is actually being spoken by the language which he thinks he is in charge of speaking for himself.

Such an emphasis on the language of the unconscious may seem at times to be mechanistic and cold. This is not entirely unexpected. Lacan thought that language belongs to the order of the symbolic. Whenever two people engage in speech to each other they are exchanging signs and will both be transformed by the process.

If transference is not just about feeling and affect, what is it about? Lacan's answer was that it is all about power. The therapist is put in the position of the one who is supposed to know. Some patients will show that they expect the therapist to have the answer to all problems but has discovered that she is not always willing to give them to the patient. Some patients go to great lengths to avoid believing that the therapist can help them and banish to the unconscious all traces of faith and hope. Nevertheless, Lacan says that the belief that there is another who does know is an indication that transference exists. This is the transference in the fundamental sense of something being transferred from one to another. One of the main problems for Lacan was his view that the transference is the act of speech itself. There is no possibility of stepping outside language in order to interpret the language that is being used. We are always encased within the language that we are using. This does not mean that there is no point in trying. It just means that there is no ultimate transference interpretation that solves all problems. Recognition of the difficulty and the need for analysis to continue throughout life may be the best that we can achieve. It would be no small achievement.

New Aspects of the Use of Transference

The first full theoretical statement of the nature and role of transference came in 'The Interpretation of Dreams' which Freud began the new century by publishing in 1900. In his model of the human mind known as *the topographical model*, the ideas that are repressed into the unconscious are not accessible to consciousness until they can form a connection with something that is conscious. An idea that is able to establish a connection to conscious material becomes preconscious. The conscious idea meanwhile acquires strength and emotional intensity from the unconscious ideas that are connected to it:

> The preconscious idea which thus acquires an undeserved degree of intensity (from the unconscious idea) may either be left unaltered by the transference or it may have a modification forced on it, derived from the idea which affects the transference. (1900: 562)

This is an immensely important development and completes the model by which ideas could pass into the unconscious and then be able to return to consciousness by means of the processes of transference. If we accept that what will be repressed will be desires, then we can see that the process of forming transference and then catching it and interpreting it in therapy will inevitably be a process of understanding the desire of the patient.

For the object relations theorists of the twentieth century, negative emotions arise when the infant is frustrated in his loving attachment to his first objects. If the first thought is the absent breast as Wilfred Bion suggested, the first hate is the object that separates the infant from its mother. That in itself broadens out the possibilities for the nature of the frustrating object.

If what comes between the child and his mother is her work or her lover, not just the child's own father, the category of objects that will be feared and resented is set well outside the limits of the father himself. The child will be concerned with his love for his mother and his need for her will determine initially the strength of that desire. The early birth of the human infant, long before he can stand or in any way fend for himself, explains why the need for the mother will be total. Freud did not invent the idea of unconscious process but he did show how it could be used in the clinic to give understanding. There is still a long way to go from understanding to changes in behaviour. Many clinicians in the twenty first century will have little conscious sense that they are using the work of Freud and they may in fact be reacting against his ideas. In some way, therefore, his thinking will have become part of their background.

The Road that is Opened by Transference

Freud founded a school and a clinic in which therapists are trained to work with love, hate, sex and death and all the other emotions deriving from them. He discovered that his patients spoke of love. His theory is a theory of love which can also be stated as a theory of desire. He asserted that all neurotic manifestations are elaborations of the libido and therefore the task of the psychotherapist is to track the path of desire in the individual with all its manifestations both as love and as hate. In this context, the unconscious processes are the means that the psyche can use to hide its desires from itself and others. Transference in this view is one of the devices by which we are thrown off the scent. I think that I hate or love this therapist and then I do not need to know that I am still affected by an experience of hating or loving in my earliest days. So why do I bring those experiences back at all in any form? Freud's answer is in the wound that they have inflicted. A wound needs to be healed, not just hidden from the air. In fact it will not heal unless it is able to access oxygen. For this reason my old pain is manifested over and over again until I understand what it is about perhaps with the help of a clinician.

This hypothesis has received support and observational validation not only from the anecdotal treasury of psychoanalysis itself but also from the work of some of the neuroscientists such as Alan Schore (2003) and the attachment theorists such as Sue Gerhardt (2004) which I shall consider in Chapter 5.

Some analytic clinicians would limit their definition of transference to the emotions that occur in relation to the therapist in the consulting room. It may be used as a technical term for those emotions which the therapist herself can see are inappropriate to the person of the practitioner but are passionately and intensively applied to him or her. Freud was interested in transference love and would perhaps have been surprised to see how his descendants have believed anger to be more often repressed than sexuality. The belief that we no longer dare express anger has led to the current fashion among some forms of counselling to be constantly seeking anger: 'I think you are angry with me' says the well meaning counsellor who thinks it is her job to *give permission to be angry*'. From this belief we have the idea that 'It's OK to be angry' and this therapy, which may sometimes be useful, but ignores the purposive aspect of transference.

Conclusion

Above all, this chapter has shown that we learn from examining the theory of transference and counter-transference that the therapist must work continuously to see where her own feelings are just that, her own feelings. On the other hand, much of what she feels but cannot account for in terms of her own life, she will be able to understand as a communication from the client. Using this communication to help the client rather than throwing it back defensively or aggressively in an effort to avoid the unpleasant feelings, is the skill that we continually seek to improve. This is never easy because it requires humility and the willingness to be wrong. It also requires willingness to change and to change before the patient can. This may require of the therapist the willingness to forgive and to tolerate the most painful feelings of anger, resentment and humiliation.

Discussion Points

A woman called Anne is seeing a male therapist because of her difficulty in making decisions at work. She develops a strong positive idealisation of the therapist, telling him that she never trusted a man before but she trusts him to lead her to the changes that she needs to make. She comes back from the first holiday break and says that she has decided to divorce her husband. What might the therapist's reaction be both in his own mind and to the patient?

1. What might be the problem with making major decisions during therapy?
2. What right does a therapist have to tell a patient what he should or should not do in his external life?
3. Can we help a patient to understand his own desire without creating a selfish monster?
4. Describe a recent session and try to distinguish your transference to the patient from your counter-transference.

3 Family Patterns

Questions to Consider While Reading

1. What do we mean by the father transference?
2. Why should we consider sibling transference?
3. What patterns are left by abusive experience?

Introduction

The first two chapters have taken account of the way in which early experience enables the child to form patterns of experience which become patterns of expectation. These patterns will be applied to new situations and may be helpful or may be counter productive. This chapter will look at the specific experience of the family structure and ways in which these patterns may be reproduced and projected onto new relationships, objects and situations in the present.

Most of the early work on the use of transference patterns focussed on the baby's relationship with the mother. We can see that the developmental stages of oral, anal and genital development will be experienced in connection with the main care giver who, for most children in Europe and the Americas will be the mother. Whether this is the case or not, other family members are of increasing importance to the growing child. D. W. Winnicott (2006: 83) expressed the importance of the mother to the small infant by his well known epigram that there is no such thing as a baby. Mother and baby are so closely intertwined and inter dependent that there cannot be a baby on its own. There is always a baby and a primary care giver, usually a mother. Where is the father and what is his role if that is the case?

Roles of father and mother in the life of a growing child are partly determined by the social context and the social ethos of the community in which the child grows up, partly by the personality of each actual parent and partly by his own internal state which, in turn is formed by processes of introjection and projection. In the twentieth century in Europe, men were often taken away from the family by the two major wars and women were left to do their best on their own. Male and female roles were strongly stereotyped. Women were still expected and sometimes compelled to give up work when they married in the first half of the century. These factors may have contributed to the emphasis in the twentieth century on the role of the mother in the work of writers such as Melanie Klein.

The father's role for D. W. Winnicott, writing in the first half of the twentieth century, is to hold the mother so that she can hold the baby. If that were the whole story, the baby would not need to see his father and would be aware only that his mother was safe and confident. He can protect the mother from having to pay too much attention to the outside world when she just wants to make a circle with her arms to keep her baby safe (1964: 25). This is a function which Winnicott thought would transmit confidence and what he called 'social security' to the baby long before he has any idea that he has two parents. The baby does, however, have to come to recognise that he does have two parents and that he cannot have his mother all to himself. This is one of the most crucial discoveries for the growing baby: the father brings not only distant security but also the warning bell that tolls for the end of the blissful mother with baby unity. The father, representing the outside world and the mother's other interests and concerns, will gradually loom into view if he is there to be seen. If there is no father, aspects of the mother's own life will appear to the child to intervene between him and her and his wishes for her total attention. If the father is there, he becomes all sorts of different things depending on his nature and the relationship between him and the mother of the child. He may envy her; he may as Winnicott points out, think that he could be a better mother than she can be. Men hide and disguise their envy of women in various ways but they are in reality deprived of the whole experience of gestation and child birth with its pain, suffering and eventual reward. They do not have an equivalent unique experience in biology since women also experience sexual arousal and climax in a way that is different but does not seem to lack the urgency and intensity of the male experience. Women then experience envy of the power and dominance which the man may assume in order to hide his own envy and sense of inferiority. Envy plays a part in the mental structures of both sexes because each individual is only male or only female and cannot know what it is to be the other.

The man as father has to construct his own role. He is not biologically essential after he has impregnated the woman. He may leave to the mother all the close contact of feeding, cleaning and washing. She may wish to keep it all for herself and not allow the father to share in these tasks. If he does not participate in the gentle touching and loving holding of the early weeks, he may enter the infant's world as the bringer of law and the wielder of discipline. Winnicott can sound dated in his culturally-related view of the tasks of mother and father, but if we take a more generalised view of the situation we can see what he means. For example there may be families in which there is a single mother who will have to do everything herself, but in the family with a father present, more help can be given by the father and tasks will usually be divided in some way even if not along the old stereotyped male and female lines.

In any family of any shape, the circle of the baby's awareness gradually increases and with it his awareness that he has to share the world with others, however unwelcome that knowledge might be,

> Every now and again the baby is going to hate someone and if his father is not there to tell him where he gets off he will hate his mother and this will make him confused because it is his mother that he loves most fundamentally.   (Winnicott, 1964: 115)

The role of the father is particularly significant in cases where the mother is ill or she is herself absent for some reason. Postnatal depression is more common than is usually understood. The serious psychotic version is rare but most women suffer the effects of shock after a normal birth and will react to the lack of sleep that follows immediately on the emotionally and physically exhausting process of giving birth. A woman's reaction to this trauma will depend of course on her own temperament and ability to contain her own feelings and will also be affected by the ability of the father to bear this state in her, just when he also has to adjust to taking second place in her concerns and her attention. His ability to tolerate the changes and to understand that some of them at least are temporary is bound to have an effect both on the mother and on the contentment of his baby.

Jacques Lacan has added a great deal to our understanding of the role of the father in bringing the outside world into the child's view. He describes the insertion of the child into the world through the acquisition of language as the process of his learning the law of the father. This is the law of our social interaction as human beings. It is the law of interaction itself and it contains the answer to narcissism. The world is not perfect and is not formed in the image that we wish to see when we look into our own mirrors. Narcissus, the beautiful youth of Greek mythology sat and stared at his own image in a woodland pool and refused to look up and see the rest of the world. He faded away and died. That is the fate of the individual who insists on seeing only the image that he imposes on his world. According to the Lacanian reading of Freud, the child must learn that there is a third term in the symbolic equation of human life. There is no longer only a baby and a mother. There is a baby, a mother and another.

When the place of the other is supplied by the father, we can turn to look at the ways in which the father is likely to have shaped the pattern of relationship to him.

> Developmental psychologists who have studied father-infant reactions have shown that the father-infant relationship is not equivalent to the mother-infant one. To start with, fathers spend less time with their infants. When they are with them, the interactions tend to be more active and exciting than the mother-infant ones.   (Marks, 2002: 99)

This observation dates from the 1960s and we might ask whether the difference is still as marked. The interactions noted then showed that men were more 'heightened and playful' when with their small infants. Mothers by contrast were more mod-ulated and smooth in their play with their infants and in any case were more likely to be carrying out the tasks of caring such as washing and feeding which were thought not to be as exciting, although later studies indicate that there is potentially excitement for both mother and child in the handling of the body and of course particularly the genitals. Much depends on the mother's attitude and emotional state. The father's interactions tend to be more overtly stimulating and unpredictable. Infants have been observed to smile and vocalise more with fathers who apparently encourage affiliative behaviour in this way. The infant prefers his mother when he is distressed. Mothers are perhaps therefore more involved with affect regulation whereas fathers or the male presence in the infant's life might be more closely connected with the regulation of social connections. The effects of these early patterns will mean that when looking for the origin of counter productive patterns in the adult, we are seeking for gender specific relationships. One important criterion of this search is not to be seduced by generalisations. The research by Marks ((2002) referred on p. 52) enables us to have some broad expectations but does not give us definitive meta patterns. Each case may be different.

All human beings in a social group have to deal with this situation for the rest of their lives and it is not unreasonable to assume that patterns will affect the individual's relationship with people in the role of the father. Most therapists have little difficulty in seeing a parallel between the role of the father and the role of the figures in authority who represent the outside world to the adult. What is more difficult is to see how the pattern of the response to the father in the past is projected in detail onto the therapist and other people in the present. Understanding this degree of detail of the life of a man is likely to be a problem for some therapists of whom the majority are women. They find it easier to place themselves in the maternal transference and the paternal projections may remain invisible.

A young man of 27, Mr P comes to see a female therapist Mrs X aged 57. His presenting problem is that he has been sent for counselling from work because he is causing difficulties at work. He has a female boss who has said that she is appointing an assistant who will become Mr P's line manger. He is very upset at what he sees as a lack of confidence in his own ability. He said 'I always did what she asked of me. Why

would she need to put in another manager above me? Why
could she not have promoted me?'

The therapist heard the reality of the problem that he had and
also began to think about the possible projections that were
making it worse. She went straight to the mother transference
because the boss was a woman and she thought that she could
assume that the mother was dominating and difficult. She had
already been told a bit of his history which substantiated this
view. His father had been a successful engineer and his mother
had stayed at home to look after the children. He had an older
brother and a younger sister and he said that being in the middle had meant that he was nobody in particular. The therapist,
working along the lines of established oedipal theory, thought
to herself that Mr P had been suffering from the existence of an
older brother who was able to have a closer relationship with
his mother. She therefore had a mind set that led her to make
interventions along the lines that he wanted to be her favourite
client. He responded to this at first by looking embarrassed and
increasingly with irritation. The therapy stalled and after a few
more sessions Mr P decided to leave.

We can never know what might have happened if the therapist
had behaved differently. Nevertheless, one aspect of the scenario
that was neglected was the presence or absence of the father.
The therapist would have had to perform the mental and emotional gymnastics of putting herself in the place of the father and
then being able to imagine how that might map onto the current situation. The boss was a woman but because she was in
the position of mediating the structures of the rest of the organisation to Mr P she was filling the role of the father figure. The
distress that Mr P felt over her actions might have related therefore to his inability to please and impress his father at least as
much as his mother. The competitiveness that the therapist was
seeking to identify might have been with the brother but might
have been for the admiration of his father.

Thinking in terms of the Oedipus complex is still helpful
because it might lead to an understanding of the difficulties with
rivalry that Mr P was experiencing. According to Freud's ideas
of the relationship of son to father, the boy needs to be able to
accept that he will not be able to outdo his father in competing

for possession of his mother. If the boy needs to be able to compete with his father, one of the roles of the father must be to allow some competition and to tolerate his son's development into a potent and successful man. In the case of Mr P, who had not had much contact with his father, we could expect that he would continue into adult life still seeking situations in which he could feel able to be admired. This might seem to be a dead end. What can Mr P hope to do about this emotional treadmill? The answer is of course that he has a real situation at work which anyone might resent and find difficult. What he can see differently is the emotional power of his reaction.

First, he must see that he could be projecting his feelings about his father onto the line manger. Second, he had begun to project those feelings onto his therapist. She did not see him as successful. On the contrary she perhaps appeared to be seeing him as a young child with his mother. Their relative ages and actual sex made this the obvious scenario. Whether he was consciously aware of his sense of humiliation, we cannot know. There is a chance that if the therapist had been able to recognise what she was doing to him, she might have been able to help with his humiliation enough to prevent his precipitous ending.

Mr M in Chapter 1 (p. 9) had a problem which his therapist understood to have arisen in relation to his experience of his father:

> A young man of 27, Mr M, comes to see a therapist because his boss has said that unless he makes some changes he will lose his job. He works as a mechanic in a car sales room. He feels that his boss, Doug, who is much older, does not understand young people. Doug, he says, comes in sometimes with a hangover and then: 'He just goes for me. I might have stayed on the night before to finish a job, and will he pay me for overtime? Once I came in late because I had had a few drinks the night before and got a bit wrecked. He started to have a go at me over something that wasn't right. Then I went for him. I didn't hit him or nothing but I swore at him. He wouldn't take that and I don't know why I did that. It was just stupid but I can't shut up now. Every time I see him it starts to come over me and I want to kill him. Why do I feel that bad? I've got to stop it.'

The listening therapist will have a variety of emotional and thinking reponses to this. She will want to help if possible and this is a trap always lying in wait because thinking about practical help, even if the decision is not to offer it, diverts us from the analytic path of understanding and elucidating which is the therapist's primary task.

In order to carry out this task, the therapist must think in the most agile and versatile way about the way in which the story of the past is projected onto present relationships.

The Absent Father

Some of the patterns that we see in adult patients relate to the experience of an absent father. This is difficult to recognise because it will be demonstrated by an attitude to the parent or carer who was present and that is most often the mother. I saw a patient who demonstrated both his feelings about his absent father and also showed that he felt scorn for his mother who had 'lost' his father and who had brought him up.

John was a successful stock market trader but was lonely and disillusioned with the sense that there was nothing more for him to achieve. He told me that he was an only child. I noticed that he told me very little about his mother but seemed to feel a mild affection for her and also to despise her mildly as not very bright. He had come to therapy because he had been looking for his father who had abandoned him and his mother when John was born. He had tracked him down but had been rejected when he turned up on the doorstep and presented himself as the long lost son. I suppose it was a great shock to the father and he was not pleased to have the potential new and disturbing element suddenly appearing in his life. John had longed for the moment and had anticipated great joy and pleasure as his father recognised him. The reality had devastated him and was of course a terrible blow to his self respect and self image.

John had always been consoled by his own intellectual ability. He had told me with great pride that he was a graduate of an old university and that he had been very popular there because he was seen as able to be 'very funny' at parties. He felt that in his working life he had lost the ability to be witty and was no longer the life and soul of any party.

The need for his father appeared in the therapy when he would ask me, as he often did, what he should do. I also felt that the father transference was present when he tried to show off to me. He had no brothers and no father to set up a competition for him when he was a child so he was still obsessed at work with winning praise from his line manager and he felt that he must stand out from the other programmers. He needed to feel that I was impressed by his brain and his success and he would lug a huge rucksack into the consulting room from which he would bring out his state of the art laptop, hand held computer and mobile phone which he sometimes accidentally left on achieving the result that I would see how popular and important he was when people rang him. Eventually there came a day when he sat sadly fingering it and saying 'no-one has rung me all day and no-one actually cares about me'. At that point I thought he was ready to change. He was able to accept his loss and acknowledge that his father was not there to be impressed.

In the second phase of his therapy, John met a girl called Kate. She was not particularly beautiful and not particularly intelligent. John told me that he met her at the pub and she was lonely. He suffered greatly at this point from the problem of Groucho Marx who would not want to belong to any club that would have him as a member. He feared that she was only interested in him because she was lonely and no one wanted her. Was this the best he could do? He made me frequently angry with him on Kate's behalf by the extent of his feeling of entitlement. Kate worshipped him, he said, and if he was so attractive to her, surely he could pull a more attractive girl? We struggled through a difficult period in which I tried to establish a link to his scornful attitude to his mother and of course to his therapist who wasn't helping him to get a better girl friend but in fact seemed to think he should be glad of the one he had found.

Thinking in terms of the relationship to the absent father helped me to maintain an analytic position with John and, in fact, to return to an awareness of how intensely painful he found it to have been abandoned by the man who could have loved him and provided him with his normal share of self esteem. While I did not see it as my job to make up for these deficits, I think that I was able to be more humane and more patient with him. I was also able to help him to reflect on his own patterns of anger and to see how they related to his underlying sadness.

The Abusive Father

I would guess that many readers when encountering this phrase would be thinking of sexual abuse. Sexual abuse is more common than anyone would wish and is, of course, at the heart of Freud's central theoretical explanation of the neurosis of women. At first he thought that the hysteric was abused by her father and has forgotten/repressed the memory of it and has fallen sick from her efforts to forget the forbidden memory. In his later writing (for example in the Introductory Lectures of 1916), he modified the belief that the sexual abuse must have actually happened as an historic event and thought instead that the girl would have unconsciously desired it as she wished to possess her father and keep him all for herself. Her own wish became the memory which must at all costs be exiled from conscious recognition. If this is the argument, we immediately encounter the natural revulsion of most ordinary people who are uninvolved with psychoanalysis. Jed Rubenfeld has written a novel about psychoanalysis and murder (*The Interpretation of Murder*, 2006) in which he gives his fictional character of Carl Jung an expression of the revulsion of his contemporaries:

> We know the grown son does not actually covet the mother sexually with her varicose veins and sagging breasts. Nor does the infant son who has no inkling of penetration. (2006: 347)

The character of Jung in the novel then proceeds to argue that the important point is to identify the conflict for the patient in the present. The infantile feeling of need is reactivated in the adult and the woman who was once of special value to him is again important in his mind and in his feelings but he need not have desired her in reality at any stage. Freud in the novel repudiates this idea passionately. For him, infantile sexuality was vital and the boy desired his mother and the girl her father.

The question of whether or not the seduction or violation that took place was a historical event or a fantasy has been the central issue in considerable debate in psychoanalysis and for feminists since then. Ann Scott (1996) has written a helpful summary of the debate that was fuelled by Geoffrey Masson (1984) in *The Assault on Truth*. She points out that only a very limited view of psychoanalytic theory would lead to an assumption that there was either a historical seduction or rape or that there was only fantasy. She argues that Masson was making the category error in his thinking of excluding the middle and that most therapists remain neutral in their attitude to the historical truth of the narrative that is presented to them:

> It is a caricature because it inscribes a view that only the most solipsistic, relativist analyst could hold, and indeed it is a view which not many analysts show signs of holding. More common is the view that there is a reality out there but the analyst's task is to enable the patient to understand how he or she is construing and misconstruing it, constructing it in such a way as to enact a role such as that of victim that the patient most wants to be free of but feels in thrall to. (1996: 16–17)

The false memory debate of the last part of the twentieth century brought out some of the difficulties of relying on memories as veridical and has shown us that there are at least two points of view to be heard on the question of the accuracy of memories, especially of long ago childhood events. See, for example, the research adduced by Sandler and Fonagy (1997).

Whatever the truth of Freud's proposition, the clinical situation that we observe often shows guilt in relation to sex. Women come to us unable to want sex with a male partner. They present themselves as lacking desire. That may well be the case but we do well to ask ourselves whether sex has been forbidden by her guilt which may be to the mother whom she feels she has betrayed in her desire for her father to love and admire only her. There are of course many other sources of *aphanisis* or loss of desire. Disgust and shame may well be left by inappropriate touching or looking by the fathers of girls. When this girl grows to a woman she may sometimes transform herself through this experience into the hysterical temptress who appears to be interested but drops the partner who trusts her encouragement. More rarely, we might find symptoms such as inappropriate interest in sex and promiscuity.

Fathers can also abuse boys sexually, but the most frequent kind of abuse of boys as well as girls is likely to be the domination and intolerance that both boys and girls can experience but which is more commonly experienced by boys. The reasons why a man is likely to shout at or hit his children are, of course, many. Sexuality of the sort mentioned in the previous section could lead to anger and an inability to tolerate either his own feelings or the presence of the girl herself as a constant reminder of what he cannot have. Boys too can suffer from this sort of aborted sexuality. More often, they suffer from a man's lack of confidence which prevents him from being able to tolerate his son's growing strength and ability and, in the end, his son's ability to surpass him. Often, the father appears to be angry with his offspring for not achieving enough. Under this apparent wish may sometimes be concealed the terror of being surpassed which says in effect: go on, show me the best you can do so that I can be sure that I can still do better. The narcissistic father may try to assume to glory of his son's achievements for himself. On the other hand, this may lead to a resolution for both of them if the father can feel that he can share in the son's achievement a little and can continue to live through it when his own active life is over. If this can be achieved by the father, the son may be helped to compete openly and energetically with people in the rest of his life as well as with his father.

Sibling Fathers

Although Freud saw siblings as rivals and therefore their place would be in the competitive areas of an adult psyche, he described the role of the siblings in a way which suggests that their role could be to represent something of the patient's feelings about the father in terms of his power and his sexual triumph over the mother:

> The elder child mistreats the younger, maligns him and robs him of his toys, while the younger is consumed with impotent rage against the elder, envies and fears him. (1900: 250)

We can see that this also occurs with sisters and that there is equal rivalry for the attention, love and admiration of either or both parents but in the first place, both sexes will seek the mother's love and approval. A little later when the father is able to become a valued presence for his child, he may be seen as a better judge and certainly as a greater challenge and therefore more desirable.

As Prophecy Coles (2003) points out, the popular view of sibling significance is restricted to rivalry. Nevertheless, any therapist knows that the relationships in the stories of incest that we hear are often stories about older brothers. She writes about the story of Isis and Osiris, who were king and queen and brother and sister. The rivalry between Isis and his brother Seth led to deaths and destruction. Seth causes his brother Osiris to be dismembered and when his wife/sister Isis puts him back together, she cannot find his penis. Somehow the brother has taken away his manhood. On the other hand, after a great struggle, Horus redeems his father. The son validates and makes the life of the father meaningful. In the end, Osiris and his son Horus manage to achieve a *modus vivendi* in which Horus ruled on the Earth as a pharaoh and Osiris rules the Underworld (2003: 23). Thus the father and son can work out their rivalry and co-exist but there is great confusion between fraternal love and hate and sexual love and hate.

Freud elaborated his theory of the repression of incestuous wishes in his paper 'Totem and Taboo' in 1913. The primitive tribes in Australia to which he alluded as evidence of the extent to which his ideas are embedded in human nature, forbid incest. He gives an explanation for the two wishes that are inherent in the Oedipus complex. Both arise from the circumstances of a small tribe with close dependence on each other and a need therefore to develop safe family relationships. The two wishes are:

- the wish to possess the mother
- the wish to kill the father.

In analytic work we can take seriously the idea that the older sibling can represent in some ways the power and authority of the father. We should therefore not be surprised that a brother can also come within the range of the oedipal wishes and the oedipal prohibition. Since this is a symbolic relationship rather than a direct and physical one, we should also not be surprised if the accounts of sibling incest are confused and often difficult to distinguish from the play and exploration in which most mixed sex siblings will indulge. The adult however is left with a sense of guilt because there is an incestuous element. Many small girls will have indulged in some kind of exploration with small boys along the lines of 'you show me yours and I will show you mine' but will not usually have been left with a feeling of either such guilt or such excitement into adulthood. For those who are left with such feelings, the therapist can provide a great deal of help in normalising the experience itself without minimising it and in allowing the guilt to have its expression and its acknowledgement.

Prophecy Coles also refers to the effect of brother sister incest on the man. She refers to Freud's account of the patient whom he called the Wolfman who had a sister two years older than he. When the parents went away for some reason and left the children alone with their nanny, his sister played exploration games with him and took hold of his penis. She was five and a half and he was three and a half. Is this an example of sexual abuse or of normal children's play? In either case, parents would forbid such activity and it takes on the mantle of that which must be secret and hidden from the outside eye. This is enough to engender a sense of guilt which could persist for the adult. Melanie Klein's own experience was perhaps more favourable than that of Freud because she pointed out that the siblings can help each other through their love and support for each other. Complicity in conspiracies against the parents can mitigate and relieve some of the power of the oedipal anxiety and defence. The five year old child known as 'Little Hans' in Freud's case history suffered his phobia of horses because, in Freud's view, of his fear that his father would take revenge because of his affectionate behaviour towards his mother. He has no siblings until his little sister is born and one could hope that as she grows older he will be able to direct some of his emotional intensity into his relationship, both good and bad, with his sister and then with a lover.

Grandparents: A Different Kind of Parenting

For the child who is lucky enough to have living grandparents, there is an opportunity to be less hurt by the necessary exclusion from the parental couple. The grandparents may be available to look after the baby at times and the occasion can be welcomed and enjoyed by both the grandparents and the children so that the parental betrayal of going out together without the child is softened or mitigated. In some cases the grandparents look after children for working parents and become substitute parents at least temporarily. On the other hand, the grandparents themselves have to face yet another reworking of their own oedipal stage. They have to face their exclusion from the parental couple which conceived the child and then continue to accept that the parent–child bond is usually quite rightly stronger than the grandparent–parent–child bond. Here too the grandparent has the opportunity to learn to live in the position of the third. Patterns will be learned in the process and old patterns reactivated.

When a woman hears that she is to become a grandmother for the first time she may well react by thinking, if not saying, 'I'm not ready; I'm not old enough'. This may be mixed with delight and pride as well as anticipation of the pleasure of being close to a baby again. Men are also likely to be faced with the reality of their age and with moving to the next generation. Men fear old age and impotence at least as much as women and may take an equally long time to reach the joy and pleasure in the new life and the life that will continue after grandparents can expect to be dead. In some cases, the pregnancy of a daughter who has been raped or abandoned will be felt as a disaster. Increasingly often the parents of teenaged girls are having to take on parenting at one remove. This may remain a problematic situation in which the arrival of a new baby is secondary to the distress and anguish of a daughter. In this situation, the grandparents will have to use whatever patterns they have of narcissistic complaint at one extreme and care and consideration for another human being at the other extreme.

Rahle Isroff (1994) described her experience of becoming a potential grandmother at the same time as one of her patients. She describes the first reactions of friends as dividing into the same two groups, expressing the lack of choice involved: 'surely you aren't old enough to be a grandmother?' and 'how wonderful, you are lucky'. Since friends are likely to be of the same generation, the potential grandmother will also encounter envy and envious attacks from those who do not have grandchildren and may not have children to give them the potential in the future.

Once a woman has begun to come to terms with the pregnancy and has accepted that it is established beyond the first three months, her feelings might follow different tracks depending on whether the baby is to be born to her daughter or daughter-in-law. Isroff writes of her experience of the baby being born to a daughter-in-law. She describes the anxiety about what to do and how to do it. Friends' advice was 'Keep your mouth shut and wear beige' (1994:260). On the surface there are all sorts of questions about how much the daughter–in-law and also the daughter will allow the grandmother to be involved or perhaps at the other end of the spectrum will want and need help and support. The pattern that will be activated will usually be the experience of one's own grandparents. They are likely to have died something like twenty to forty years before and the memories of the grandparents may be detailed or may have become softened and idealised over time. Traditions and even such details as the names used in the family will be likely to be handed on and perpetuated. Do you want to be known as Grandma or Granny, Nana or Nanny? Or do you want the child to use your first name. At this point the existence of the Other Grandmother is likely to be clearly visible to the new grandparent. Is there going to be a number one and number two grandmother and which will I be? Another potential source of jealousy and rivalry is immediately born.

The grandparents will also come up against the Oedipus situation yet again. We know that there will have been many situations for any adult in which he or she has had to deal with the third or with being in the third position. The pregnancy of a daughter or daughter-in-law presents both grandparents with the experience of the birth of a baby which is of great importance but is not their own. They need to recognise the existence of a couple from which they are excluded. The pregnancy itself is undeniable evidence that the son or daughter now has a sexual relationship and is setting up a family which may make room for a grandparent but does not allow for another parent. Of course there are the rare circumstances in which the mother is a single parent and wishes her own mother to take the role of partner. More rarely, her father may be offered the role of partner but, in either case, there will be stresses and strains which arise to some extent because it is clear to all that the grandparents are only substitute parents and there is a kind of oedipal victory in taking the place of the absent father. Guilt and anxiety will make themselves felt.

In some families the pattern of grandparental involvement may be almost totally benign and the example left in the mind of the adult may be of good relationships and a much loved old woman or man. In other cases, the grandmother or grandfather may have been seen as a nuisance who became senile or physically ill and was a problem for the parents. The child or young adult may have seen the parents arguing over how to deal with the problem created by the old age of the grandparents and may have resented them both for showing the effects of growing old and for causing disputes and disquiet in the family. Tolerance and kindness in the parents will have been a great help but may not be in the background for many people.

For most of our patients, the grandparents will have demonstrated the process of dying. This may be sudden and relatively invisible. The shock that this caused to the parents will be correspondingly great. A long drawn out illness may have been endured with dignity but will almost always have been distressing both to the parents and to the child. Nevertheless, the death of grandparents is likely to be a template for the experience that for good or ill will stay with many adults. It may help the patient to speak of fears of death or hope to be able to manage death, both their own and also death of others, particularly the death of partners which many older people dread.

A surprising number of patients speak of grandparents as having played a very important part in their childhood. The death of a grandmother who brought a patient up in the absence of a parent will of course be felt like the death of a parent and is likely to occur while the patient is younger and less able to process grief. More often, grandparents are felt to be important representations of stability and security, especially needed when parents are troubled, sick or absent. Age lends some sort of wisdom perhaps and certainly lends distance from the troubles of the child and therefore the child feels that there was some sense of proportion in the way the grandparents dealt with his problems. This may result in a pattern of willingness to consider the opinions of others and may also lead to respect for those who are different.

Grandparents can also fill any of the negative roles that parents may take on. Whatever an abusive parent may do, the grandparent may also do and there have been cases of sexual and physical abuse by grandfathers and grandmothers. Unintentional mistreatment may arise from the generational difference itself. Children are extremely sensitive to the way in which they are seen by contemporaries and grandparents may be over indulgent or over strict depending to some extent on whether they are echoing or reacting against their own childhoods. A child who is brought up by grandparents may learn patterns of concealment and avoidance of authority. This may be caused by fear of the authority of the grandparent who is feared or revered by the parents and of course the character of each individual grandparent will give rise to differing responses.

The Relationship 'In Law'

The relationship that is only 'in law' has given rise to music hall jokes in our society. In some societies, the mother-in-law is much more powerful than the mother for a girl. In many cultures such as the Hindu and some parts of the Islamic world for example, the girl has to leave her home and be ceremoniously taken to her husband's family home where she will be ruled by the new family for the rest of her life. Her mother-in-law will seek sometimes to have revenge for her own experience and for her own powerlessness through dominating her new daughter in law. In this way old patterns of abuse may be perpetuated with the willing connivance of one of the parties. If she has a son of her own, she will have the opportunity of her own revenge when he marries and she becomes a mother-in-law in her turn. Domination and exploitation can be handed on in this way.

Even in western cultures where the daughter-in-law expects to be free and independent, the relationship with the mother-in-law is made difficult if there is a contest over the man. The mother of a son may find it hard to 'give him away' to another woman, now his wife. Everything that is true of the mother-in-law of a woman is equally true of a mother-in-law of a man. In the Christian marriage ceremony, only the father is required to give away his daughter. Yet the mother has to give up just as much in accepting the importance of the new husband of her daughter. The complicated fabric of jealousy and rivalry will often make the place of the mother-in-law a difficult one to manage and may be as much a problem for her as for the younger couple:

> A son is a son till he takes a wife
> A daughter's a daughter all her life

A daughter, as the old saying goes, is likely to be still very attached to her own mother and father and this strong tie will rival the relationship with her husband. He will find that competition difficult unless he has learned patterns of tolerance and generosity in his own upbringing.

Sons and Daughters

When an older patient comes to see a therapist, he or she is bringing all the experience that has made a strong emotional imprint. An older patient will often have grown up children and for both sexes, the process of bearing and bringing up children is one of the most demanding, exciting and sometimes disturbing events of adult life. We might be surprised therefore if the patterns of experience that we find transferred to the therapist and to other adults did not include recognisable phenomena that relate to the children that they have borne and brought up. Of course these experiences themselves will be rooted in the earlier experience of caring and being cared for. Older patients with younger therapists may be approached by the route of understanding the way in which they relate to a younger relative.

One of the rare examples of an older patient presenting for therapy was provided by Mrs M:

Mrs M, a woman of 83 who came to a woman therapist of 42. Mrs M was in good health but was referred by her GP for counselling because she was lonely. She was brought to therapy by her daughter who lived nearby and seemed to feel responsible for her, but did not want her to come and live with her family. Mrs M was at first bright and optimistic, saying how good her daughter had been to her. Gradually, however after the first sessions she began to be more demanding. She wanted to change the time of the sessions to earlier in the day because she was too tired in the afternoon. Her therapist thought that might be quite reasonable for someone of her age and did find another time. Then she wanted a chair that was more comfortable for her back which she had not mentioned before. Again the therapist thought that she should agree as she was dealing with an older person. After this happened, the material that was brought to the next session was a story about how Mrs M's mother always assumed that Mrs M would run round to a neighbour when she needed to borrow something that she needed for a recipe. Her mother loved cooking but often found herself halfway through a recipe without an essential ingredient. She sent Mrs M who was the youngest child to ask for it. Mrs M hated asking but said that she had developed 'a thick skin' so that her mother would not be disappointed when 'she so much wanted to make the cake or the biscuits for us'. She said that she overcame her fear of the neighbours 'but I might have seemed a bit rude to them. I wanted to get it over with'.

The therapist heard all this and merely commented that asking is difficult but that maybe it is always easier to ask a younger person to do something for you. Mrs M then began to talk about her daughter and how much she would like to be asked to live in her house. 'I can't ask her though because she has so much to do.' After several months of therapy, Mrs M decided that she could manage with the time that her daughter was able to give her even though it was never going to seem like enough. At that point she herself recognised the transference pattern and said 'I make demands on people when I'm scared, like when I was little. I don't need to be so scared any more because I'm as grown up as I'm going to get'.

Mrs M reminds us that no matter how old a person is and how long ago the pattern was established, there remains a possibility of recognising the feelings and with that recognition, being able to change. In all the work that this book has considered, the hope is that this will happen. Each person needs the courage to face their own truth and only in doing so can they achieve freedom from the constraints of their early family patterns. This chapter has considered some of the less usual aspects of family patterns that can be transferred into the therapeutic relationship. The therapist needs to look at the whole of the situation that is brought and consider how she may be able to help through identifying the patterns that are still prevailing and still causing unthinking behaviour like that of Mrs M.

Conclusion

Transference patterns are established through every relationship that the growing child and adult makes. This chapter has looked at some of the less obvious areas of transference in the family relationships which extend our thinking beyond the relationship with the primary care giver which is usually the mother. A therapist who wishes to make good use of an understanding of transference patterns will need to be looking out for the way in which the patient has encountered his father, siblings, grandparents, aunts and uncles. People outside the family can also be sufficiently important to have led to the establishment of patterns. Teachers, mother's 'friend' who came round often when father was not there, not to mention step parents will all need to be considered when they form part of the story that is told.

Discussion Points

Mrs N is a Muslim woman from Pakistan who comes to see a white British woman therapist at her GP's suggestion. She presents with the difficulties she is having with her husband's family. She is thinking of running away but does not know where she would go or how she would live. The therapist is shocked when she discovers that the marriage was forced and Mrs N has been beaten for disobeying her mother-in-law. The therapist begins to wonder whether Mrs N's life would be at risk if she ran away.

1. What problems will this therapist face in keeping a neutral stance with Mrs N?
2. What are the problems facing a therapist brought up in twentieth/twenty first century Britain in working with an adult who has grown up in a different culture?
3. How have you seen abuse whether sexual, verbal or physical affecting an adult patient?
4. What can the therapist do in the case of abuse without running the risk of becoming an accessory to family break up?

4 How Does the Use of the Transference Concept Help Clinicians?

Questions to Consider While Reading

1. What is meant by the required relationship and how can a therapist work with it?
2. What is meant by:

   Introjection?
   The superego?

3. What use is the concept of projective identification?

The first three chapters considered the theoretical underpinning of the concept of transference. Recognising the patterns formed by all the varieties of human experience contributes to the validation of the theoretical underpinning of the transference concept. Because transference is essentially a clinical concept, Chapter 4 will consider the specific ways in which therapists can use an understanding of the patterns of the past to help people to escape from counterproductive cycles of thought and behaviour and move on to facing what is in front of them in the present.

Sooner or later, anyone hoping to be of use to people suffering from mental distress will have to face the question: does what I do actually help? In supervision, many therapists show that they are genuinely concerned because the process of therapy can be slow and the results are not easily measurable. Patients may also have reasons for not letting the therapist know about any improvements. Latent anger with the parents will prevent a patient from wanting the authority figure who takes their place from having the satisfaction of a job well done. Envy will also affect the patient's ability to give anything to the therapist/parent who already seems to have so much. These are some of the reasons for the negative therapeutic reaction described in Chapter 1. The patient may also be strongly attached to the therapist and may fear that admitting that he is better may lead her to suggest an ending. In fact, the patient who is suffering because he is not able or willing to reflect on his own mental state may not be aware of changes in the level of suffering that he is experiencing.

Since listening is the first essential for working with any new patient, the therapist will listen before doing anything else. She is likely to use facilitative interventions that encourage the expression of the patient's feelings and thoughts. Even in the first session, some therapists will want to make a trial intervention of the sort that they believe to be therapeutic in order to test the patient's ability to understand and use what she can offer (Murdin 2005). Sometimes there will be enough material for the therapist to attempt a connection between two figures where transference patterns seem to be operating. More often, she will point to something that the patient says about the past as an explanation for feelings and thoughts that are present in the room such as anxiety about speaking to a stranger. Most likely the first intervention is linking two ideas or experiences to see whether or not the patient can see the point of connecting ideas together. This is a vital skill for anyone who is to be able to make some use of transference work. The following illustration shows how a therapist might work with her experience:

> Ms S sought therapy because she was unhappy in the work that she was doing at a checkout in a supermarket. She wanted to train as a nurse but was a single parent with a child of 6 and she said that she was worried that the demands of the training would harm her daughter. She had been awarded a place on a training course for mature applicants. She had originally begun a degree course but had dropped out when she discovered that she was pregnant. The father of the child was still in touch but did not live with her. Her GP had suggested that she should seek therapy when she described her level of anxiety to him.

In the first session she talked about the difficulties that she was experiencing in attending the course. Her daughter, Chloe, had asthma and was liable to suffer from chest infections and had to be kept at home when she did. The only help that Ms S could find was from her ex-partner, Rae, who was the child's father but she was worried that he was not sensitive enough to the child's needs and would take her out in the cold so that he could go and meet his mates in the day. She said little about her own past and seemed to be totally focussed on getting the therapist to give her advice on how to find better childcare. Alternatively, maybe she should give up her course and resign herself to staying at the supermarket until her daughter was in secondary school. She said that if she had to do that it would be 'a living death'.

The therapist was disturbed by this session. We can assume that she would have reported to her supervisor that she did not know how she was going to be able to help Ms S. In the hypothetical supervision session, the supervisor suggested that maybe she would have to change the emphasis to the discovery of how Ms S could help herself with the help of therapy. Nevertheless, both acknowledged that without much understanding of Ms S's background, it would be difficult to make any meaning of the dilemma in which she found herself. In addition, there was great concern expressed by both that the situation was about the danger to the child and that this would have to receive constant attention.

The therapist made a link in the first session for Ms S:

You were left alone to have your baby and bring her up. You seem to be worried about leaving your daughter alone now in the same way.

To this Ms S replied:

Well I could look after myself but she is too young and I don't trust him.

The link was at least heard although the patient made a reasonable rejection of it. The therapist began to hope that Ms S might be able and willing to consider other links that might be made in the future and that this approach might help this patient. She is showing a common kind of resistance, however, in that she seems to hear the therapist's intervention as a criticism that she has to answer.

Ms S continued to attend therapy and in the first sessions described some of the complaints that the staff and students were making about her absences. She spoke about her partner Ray and described how he would not talk to her about her daughter but simply picked her up and dropped her off again. After six weekly sessions, she said that she was anxious that she would be thrown off the course and that she could not see how the therapy was helping her. The therapist became very anxious in turn: 'how can I let her continue to come to see me when she can't even afford child care?'

This apparently ethical question raises several problems, however the first question was addressed by the supervisor:

S: Do you think that she or the child would be better off if you said that you would not see her any more?

T: Well, I think she would feel that I had abandoned her. But I want to know that it's more than just that I don't harm her by continuing.

S: Perhaps you are feeling like Ms S. She is anxious that Ray just picks up and drops off her daughter without paying proper attention. She is afraid that Sophie is neglected or even damaged by the process I think?

T: Yes. And I am also worried that I can't protect her and help her enough which is what worries her about Sophie. I wish I knew more about her background so that I could trace this back.

The therapist did not know very much about the family background of Ms S. She had been so concerned to tell the story of the course and her daughter that there had been no time for any questions about the past. The therapist had felt completely justified in listening carefully without too much probing.

Some weeks later, the therapist became worried because Ms S was telling about how she'd used a dating agency's chat room. She met a man once for a drink and did not like him. He then continued to e-mail her asking for photographs and giving long descriptions of how he imagined that she might look if she were naked. The patient seemed to feel very ambivalent about this, partly enjoying his interest and partly aware that this was a completely unknown person who might be dangerous.

The therapist became anxious that the patient and even her daughter could be harmed and she ought to be able to prevent any harm if she took appropriate action. She was not sure what this action might be and wanted the supervisor to tell her. After discussing the reality of the position of the child, the supervisor recommended that the mother should be encouraged to think about the child's safety and to go to the police if she were at all worried. The main task was to help Ms S to find the root of her own need to run risks with safety and to begin to understand what she was repeating from her own past with her child. She had described a mother who was completely unable to deal with her father and Ms S seemed to have reconstructed every aspect of the pervious scenario except for one essential difference. She had come to see the therapist and had told her what was happening. The therapist was able to change the story by thinking about what was going on and seeing how the present structure was rooted in the past. Only when that was established, was the therapist able to feel that that her work was effective for both mother and child. As soon as the therapist began to work on this aspect of the patient's material, the dangerous enmeshment with the dating agency's chat room stopped and Ms S began to lay down boundaries for Rae.

The supervisor, of course, could not and would not give definitive answers to the therapist's desperation but did help her to take up the client's own apparent anxiety which in turn helped the client to recognise that she was partly attracted by the risk. Like the father in the family, whose role can be seen as holding the mother who holds the baby, the supervisor's role may often be to hold the therapist who holds the patient. In addition, the supervisor saw that his own response was in some sort of transference connection with the client. He wanted to be able to prevent this woman and her child from coming to harm and, in so doing, to become the protective mother or father whom she seemed to be constantly seeking. Pointing out this parallel in supervision enabled the therapist to see that she was being put into the *required transference*.

The Required Transference

The concept of *required transference* is a development of the work of Melanie Klein who took the clinical use of the ideas arising from the concept of transference much further. Her work with small children caused shock and anxiety in her contemporaries but it gave rise to a view of transference which had much greater depth and resonance than before. Klein's contemporaries found her analysis of children, such as the boy she called Peter, very difficult to hear but her work in connecting the adult's mental state to childhood brings with it the great emphasis that she put on the body:

> At the very beginning of his first session Peter took the toy carriages and cars and put them first one behind the other and then side by side, and alternated this arrangement several times. In between he took two horse-drawn carriages and bumped one into another, so that the horses' feet knocked together, and said: 'I've got a new little brother called Fritz.' I asked him what the carriages were doing. He answered: 'That's not nice,' and stopped bumping them together at once, but started again quite soon. Then he knocked two toy horses together in the same way. Upon which I said: 'Look here, the horses are two people bumping together.' At first he said: 'No, that's not nice,' but then, 'Yes, that's two people bumping together,' and added: 'The horses have bumped together too, and now they're going to sleep.' Then he covered them up with bricks and said: 'Now they're quite dead; I've buried them.' In his second session he at once arranged the cars and carts in the same two ways as before – in a long file and side by side; and at the same time he once again knocked two carriages together, and then two engines – just as in the first session. He next put two swings side by side and, showing me the inner and longish part that hung down and swung, said: 'Look how it dangles and bumps.' I then proceeded to interpret. Pointing to the 'dangling' swings, the engines, the carriages and the horses, I said that in each case they were two people – Daddy and Mummy – bumping their 'thingummies' (his word for genitals) together. He objected, saying: 'no, that isn't nice', but went on knocking the carts

together, and said: '*That's* how they bumped their thingum-
mies together.' Immediately afterwards he spoke about his
little brother again.... (Klein 1975: 182)

A possible objection to this approach might be that Klein was
bringing her adult consciousness of sexuality to her work with
children and imposing on them ideas that they could not possibly
have at their age. Whatever you might think about it, her ideas
led to a conviction in many adult analysts and therapists that the
basis of our unconscious is indeed, as Freud said, the affairs of
the body. Even if you restrict the reality to the nipple entering
the mouth of the baby and the faeces leaving her anus, an image
of entering and leaving and its emotional correlative is primary
to all human life. In our unconscious desires, anxieties and fears,
we are all concerned with connection, contact and things going
in and out of openings.

Klein herself was very explicit in her work with adults too,
using references to breasts and penises to an extent that is easy to
caricature. Most counsellors and psychotherapists are now more
likely to talk about more general functions: taking in, swallow-
ing, listening, thinking, evacuating. We have adapted perhaps for
the sake of the patients, perhaps for our own sake or perhaps for
the public image of analysis.

Although, for the purposes of once weekly and shorter term
work, therapists may have moderated the shocking effect of
Klein's bodily imagery, we have retained the emphasis on the
importance of finding the bodily origin of the image that disturbs
the adult patient. What is it that left Ms S so anxious about the
contact between her daughter and her partner and what made
her invite dangerous contact with her dates? Would we be able
to trace her own anxieties back to her parents' behaviour and the
fears that she developed over the coming together of mother and
father? This kind of anxiety would be called *transference* because
it is applying an image to the present where it has no direct
relevance except through a link made outside of the patient's
awareness.

Klein did not stop at this revolutionary view of the use of
transference, she went further, taking the extended consequences
of this idea, saying that what is transferred into the analytic relationship is not so much the actual relationship that existed with

a particular person of the past, but the patient's retained image of the relationship which might be completely unrecognisable to anyone else. Actual experience might have played some part in it but would have been mixed with other unconscious images and processes to give rise to phantasy. By definition, mental contents are constantly altered and affected by the ongoing processes of projection, re-introjection, and re-projection. This is a useful reminder that these processes do not stop but continue like the growing of hair or teeth, silently and without conscious awareness but nevertheless constantly. Because of the process of *introjection* there is gradual change to what has been internalised. The pattern that appears today cannot be an exact replica of what happened in the past twenty or thirty years before.

Introjection

For Melanie Klein, the process of learning to live in the world, for the baby, is dominated by the twin processes of introjection and projection (see p. 82). As the baby literally takes in food, she also takes in experiences of the world outside her own body. These experiences have an emotional tone to them and leave a residue in the mind (Klein 1974: 244). This residue will begin to form a pattern and the pattern is a template for interpreting future experiences that are similar. Klein wrote about the need to help patients to become less anxious about the contents of the mother's body in order to become less anxious about their own bodies. The children she saw responded well to her interpretations that they were anxious about sex and intercourse between bodies as well as about the ownership of the feeding breast. When these anxieties were spoken in words, and a much calmer adult view of the body was conveyed by Klein herself to the child, the former terrifying introjects could be rendered harmless.

An example of this is given in her work with the child whom she called John, aged seven (Klein 1931). He suffered from various neurotic symptoms and intellectual inhibitions which we might call learning difficulties. Klein treated him for about two years before the account which she gives of two particular sessions in which she was able to get at the introjections that seemed to have caused him to be inhibited. He came one day saying that he was going to turn out his drawer in the play room. In it he found all sorts of rubbish that he had put in there. On the same day at home he looked in another drawer and found his fountain pen. Klein says that he was able to look into his mother's body and restore it and, more importantly perhaps, had looked into his own body and found his penis. Symbolically, he had found his own potency and had acquired less dread of what he had done to his mother.

Klein always emphasises the importance of parallel processes in the mind and body. When the mind is able to conceive of a less anxious and destructive inside that is because the outside has enabled and facilitated this change. Similarly, when things change in the mind, the projections will be less dangerous and damaging and there will be less destructive introjection as a consequence. What does all that mean for the process in the work with patients? It could imply that we are carrying out a process of making up for the deficits of childhood with the implication that we should show love for the patient and perhaps physical holding would be indicated.

In fact, this was not Klein's own view, nor that of those who have followed and used what she taught. R.D. Hinshelwood in *Clinical Klein* (1994) makes clear throughout that one purpose of therapy is to enable the introjection of a good object which might be a thinking mind (ibid. 1994: 71). This is one of the most crucial aspects of working with transference patterns. The therapist models and demonstrates that the impossible misery of the neurotic can be given thought and that thought will make a difference. Klein's thinking developed the symbolising function as a specialised form of thinking which she believed that everyone needs to be able to use. In particular we need to be able to think symbolically about the inside of the mother's body. That is where conception, the fruitful joining together of two people takes place. When two people have been able to join together fruitfully, a baby can be conceived and the baby can be sheltered and enabled to grow.

The importance of the symbolic union of the parents can hardly be overestimated. All our human relationships depend on this template that says that I can dare approach another person who is as different from me as it is possible to be, that is, of the opposite sex, and that there will be risk and challenge and creativity but ultimately the potential for some new life. This image is widely used in human communication and can hardly escape being of importance in the consulting room. It is in fact the central image of relationship and of the dignity and value of difference and of both sexes and by implication of other forms of human difference in race, nationality, class, language, age, etc.

There are many examples of the application of Klein's ideas to the work with a patient but the use of the idea of symbolism is one of the most widespread. It is also open to abuse. The therapist who is too authoritarian can state categorically that a patient means that when he is talking about performing in public he is actually talking about masturbating in public. This kind of statement may have its place but must be tentative until the patient shows that it is appropriate and useful. It should always be closely based in the material that the patient has already brought.

Robert Caper (1998) has described the process of dream analysis in a way which demonstrates the application of Klein's use of the transference to help us to understand the unspoken and unspeakable thought in the dream. The following extract shows Caper's approach:

She was in New Zealand. She was travelling through the interior. She knew that she was a foreigner there and she was allowed to travel through the country but wasn't allowed to settle there. As she drove along she wondered what would happen if the car broke down. She was in a wood and there were people there who seemed to be blue. They looked almost as if they were the trunks of trees but they were actually people. They were the native people. She knew that there was some idea that she ought not to disturb them, that they were very primitive but they had their own lives and their own way of doing things, their strange customs, which shouldn't be disturbed. Then she saw one of them lying down in the road and she thought to herself, 'I must be careful. I mustn't kill that one.' That was the end of the dream.

Although I did not say so directly to my patient, I found this dream very moving. In a compressed and visual form it conveyed her conception of the experience of analysis, including its imminent ending, but beyond that the dream seemed to

link this situation with earlier, sensual, pre-verbal experiences, probably originating in infancy, perhaps concerned
with observing and being observed. I thought that she did not
literally remember these experiences, but unconsciously felt
them to be alive in the present as feelings in her inner world –
the kind of experience that Klein describes as 'memories in
feeling' (Klein, 1957).

I asked why did she think it was New Zealand and she said
she'd no idea. I said I thought 'New Zealand' meant 'new-
seeing-land', and she laughed. (She had occasionally described
analysis as a new way of seeing things.) 'It was a strange
dream,' she went on to say, 'and I think it's about the world
inside my mind, inside mine and perhaps yours too, the
strange world I have been in here. Just the way it actually
is, I'm allowed to visit but I can't stay permanently.'

I agreed and went on to say that this strange land with its
primitive people was an attempt to describe her feeling not
only about her analysis and about me, but about the way,
as she'd said, she felt about the 'interior', the inside of my
mind. These were the thoughts and people inside me that
gave me my particular character and individuality and that
made it possible for me to give her something that was different from what she could give herself. It was as if I had a
sort of intercourse with these strange beings, an intercourse
whose outcome was valuable to her, but which at the same
time made her feel angry, even murderous. (I was thinking
at this moment in the session, perhaps too explicitly, about
the strange wood as an internal version of the primal scene
with herself as observer which Britton (1989) describes as
'triangular space'.)   (Caper 1998: 210)

This extract from Caper's clinical material shows several of
the processes of pattern identification in practice. He is on the
look out for clues about the patient's symbolising process and
from what that tells him about what she is feeling and transferring from the past into the current situation with him. He is
very focussed when he seeks to squeeze the full meaning from
'New Zealand' by associating it with seeing. The patient might
still not find any of this useful and might have her own views and

the therapist must always be prepared to be found wrong. Nevertheless, he presents something to her which gives her something to chew on and either swallow or spit out.

The process of offering interpretations becomes a matter of offering a tentative piece to a jigsaw that might make sense but might make the wrong sense or no sense at all. The wrong sense is always the more dangerous because it is attractive to both patient and therapist to complete the puzzle with the one piece that is still missing.

Leaving any puzzle without solving it is highly unsatisfactory and transference interpretations always begin as a puzzle. If there is no puzzle, there is no need for the therapist to arrive at an understanding. Some further considerations of the requirements of the art of interpretation need to be added. Elizabeth Bott Spillius demonstrates that Klein did not think any transference interpretation is complete if it only refers to the 'here-and-now' of the session (Melanie Klein Archive, CPP/KLE/C59):

> She thought the analyst should link the present up to the phantasies and if possible to the realities of the remembered past. This approach led, I believe, to a less explanatory sort of analysis and to richer and more varied clinical work. So, where Freud had at first made didactic explanations to his patients and then began to stress the role of transference and to use it as evidence for his deductions and reconstructions, Klein carried this trend further, focusing even more than Freud on the analyst/patient relationship, but not, perhaps, as much as many analysts do today.   (Spillius: 2000)

Spillius helpfully raises the question of how the analyst is to think about what goes on in the here and now of the session and how that is to be linked to the unconscious phantasy of the body. In order to make use of the ideas of transference in Klein's sense, the therapist must use several others of Klein's clinical concepts.

Projection and Projective Identification

These two concepts are in many ways the hallmark of Klein's work and are essential to most clinical applications of transference. Charles Rycroft (1968) defined projection with reference to Freud. First the subject comes across an unacceptable aspect of himself. For example, Dr Schreber (see also Chapter 1, p. 21) found homosexual attraction unacceptable. He has an unconscious impulse to get rid of the unacceptable feeling. Reversing the feeling is another form of protection to disguise it more effectively. In Schreber's case the process became:

> I don't love him, I hate him
> But
>
> If I don't love him there is no reason to hate him therefore
>
> I don't hate him he hates me.

This transformation illustrates the process by which fear can lead to paranoia. Schreber's own fear led him to believe that the object of his homosexual love was actually the one who did the hating.

Charles Rycroft (1968) defined projection by its Latin origin as the throwing of an image arising from one's self onto another object whether a person or an inanimate object. The thrower then reacts to the object as though it were the object that was generating the feelings. This is a very useful defence against experiencing what is painful and therefore one which most of us frequently employ. Both careful analysis and then courage are needed to enable a subject to see that he is projecting and that he thinks he sees in another is the hate that originally emanates from him. Schreber was in no state to recognise the probable truth of his paranoia and we do not fully understand the mental condition and its relationship to physiology. Many patients find this sort of interpretation unwelcome and often unacceptable. Therapists can easily cause the premature ending of a therapy by a too zealous or overly early attempt to analyse what appear to be projections.

Transference as Projection

Trainees in training often ask: Is projection transference? The answer to that is only 'probably.' The other way round though, we could say with certainty that transference is always projection. If a figure from the past is projected onto a person in the present and then reacted to as though he were that figure, that is transference via projection.

It is important to stress that Klein thought of projective identification as the patient's *phantasy*. In cases of projection by a patient into the analyst, Klein thought that the analyst should not be emotionally affected by the projection. If the analyst *were* affected, Klein thought it was because the analyst was not working properly. But Wilfred Bion, in particular, began to show how a patient's projection might affect the analyst emotionally and how, if the analyst understood what was happening correctly, he could use his own emotional responses as a source of information about the patient. In *Language and the Schizophrenic* (Bion 1955), for example, he gives a striking illustration of a session with a psychotic patient in which, although the patient at first seemed calm, Bion felt a growing fear that the patient would attack him. He interpreted that the patient was pushing into his insides the patient's own fear that he would attack Bion. The tension in the room then lessened, but the patient clenched his fists. Bion then interpreted that the patient had taken his fear of murdering Bion back into himself, and was now afraid that he might actually make a murderous attack on Bion.

Projective Identification

This is one of the most difficult theoretical concepts to use in a way that is helpful to the patient rather than only to the therapist. It has an element of the occult in it or perhaps just that which we do not yet properly understand. Somehow, the patient who is on the brink of experiencing unacceptably painful feelings ejects them into the therapist or any other person who is present. The therapist then experiences the feelings as if they were her own and the patient reacts as though being hit by the anger or resentment or bitterness which the therapist is experiencing. The patient in this way communicates his feelings to the analyst who must process them and express them in an acceptable and useful form. This process can set up one of the most negative and difficult interpersonal systems that we encounter.

Too much use of this concept to explain away unpalatable feelings by the analyst makes for vivid analysis but is of course susceptible to error and misuse. The dangers are that the analyst will be overwhelmed by the patient's projection and will become unable to think, or that he will refuse to take in the projected emotion, or that he will get caught up in some form of mutual acting out with the patient such as mutual idealisation or a sadomasochistic encounter. The basic difficulty for the analyst, as Money-Kyrle describes it, '... is in differentiating the patient's contribution from his own' (Money-Kyrle 1956). Klein herself thought that to remain sane, the analyst must remember that the feelings belong to the patient but too much reliance on the idea of projective identification as the patient's phantasy would lead analysts to blame patients for their own deficiencies and mistakes. This is only one of the paradoxes that the analytic therapist must accept and continually re-work in her own mind and practice.

This is the reason why there is a risk in adopting Paula Heimann's idea of widening the notion of counter-transference to include all the analyst's emotional responses to the patient and using them as a source of information about the patient (Heimann 1950). And, indeed, although I think the use of the ideas of projective identification and counter-transference have greatly enriched our understanding of the analytic relationship; we also need to be aware of the dangers of getting preoccupied with monitoring our own feelings to the detriment of direct contact with the patient's material.

Projective identification and counter-transference are two concepts that still predominate as tools for understanding the patterns that we see in interpersonal expression. Taken together, they have greatly influenced our view of the analyst/patient relationship and have led us to seek increasingly to understand the actions of the patient, his unconscious pressures, sometimes gross, sometimes very subtle, to get the analyst to feel certain feelings, think certain thoughts, act in certain ways. All this has become as important, sometimes more important, than the actual verbal content of sessions. This emphasis, sometimes described as focus on 'enactment' by patient and analyst, has been particularly important in the work of Betty Joseph (1989), who describes in a series of technical papers how patients constantly 'nudge' their analyst to behave in accordance with the patient's unconscious phantasies and expectations. This is Joseph's way of describing what Joseph Sandler calls 'actualisation' (Sandler 1976a, 1976b). Joseph tends to focus on the immediate analyst/patient relationship first before linking it with the patient's view of his past (Joseph 1985), but this is a topic on which there is considerable variation from analyst to analyst (Spillius 1988, Vol. 2, pp. 15–16). The theory of projective identification gives rich opportunities for forming interpretations that seek to give back the projections to the patient:

> Ms J is seeing a therapist because she has a very poor relationship with her husband. She has not had intercourse with him for five years and she has formed an attachment to another man. When she comes to her session she nearly always manages a pseudo orgasm at some point in the session in which she shouts and rages at the therapist who is useless and does not understand her needs. The therapist dislikes being shouted at in this way and is worried about the other people using the house. The therapist tolerates a few outbursts of this sort and then begins to feel really angry. In her own mind she is thinking: 'what does she want from me? She says I don't understand her but what is there to understand? She doesn't tell me anything. No wonder her husband doesn't want to come near her'. Because she is well trained she keeps control of her temper but she does say to the patient: 'you are making me feel useless because you feel useless. You think that you are no good.' After this the patient explodes in further anger, walks out of the session and does not return.

The therapist was trying to use her counter-transference but had not paid enough attention to the narcissistic disturbance in this patient. Any intervention might of course have led to the same outcome. Nevertheless, thinking of the patient's anxiety about not being loved, the therapist might have tried to pay more attention to the judgment in her words and to the rejection that she might have been thought to be issuing. Certainly she said 'you think that you are no good' but the patient may not have heard the qualification which is intended to convey that it is not her own view. Perhaps the fear could be brought more to the fore:

'you fear that you are no good and this prevents you from being able to risk letting me be any good'. This is dangerous ground and any such intervention is liable to rouse unmanageable anger.

Transference and the Superego

Another way of relating transference patterns to the work with a patient is through the mutative interpretation described by James Strachey (1934). He saw patients dominated by patterns of relationship which he described as the 'primitive superego'. He was asking an important question, not only

'To whom is the patient talking?'

but also

'To whom is the patient listening?'

Therapists of all denominations will ask questions like this when they hear language that speaks of commands and prohibitions: I must, I must not, I ought to, I ought not to, etc. Of course we all need prohibitions and instructions and there is no value in trying to remove them. What might be valuable is helping a patient to understand the assumption on which he bases his relationships.

The Superego and Evidence-based Living

What exactly is the superego? Freud described one of the *agencies* of his structural model as carrying the remnants of the Oedipus complex which for boys and men forbids intercourse with the mother, threatening castration for the boy who persists. It is an instrument of social control because it comes into operation at around the time when the child is accepting that mother and father have each other and he will have to find his own partner when he is big enough. The superego function will usually take on some aspects of the parental voices but is not most usefully thought of as the simple echo of parental authority. Strachey points out that it can be cruel and vindictive or peremptory and demanding and it can lie at the base of psychosis when its commands are not recognised as internally generated.

In any case, the patient may be helped by examining his own superego function and the way in which it relates to his personal ethics and his interpersonal relationships as well as for his own self-image. The answer to the question above is just as likely to be that he is listening to himself as that he is listening to another. He has internalised prohibition and a terrible price is to be paid for non-conformity. School and training, early work experiences will all reinforce the belief that some behaviour is accepted and some is punished. Each individual will deal with this in his own way but his internal model will affect every aspect of his life.

Strachey's formulation of the mutative interpretation as the vehicle of the therapeutic action of psychoanalysis reflects the importance that he ascribed to this area of mental function. He considered what makes a mutative interpretation work and what makes it difficult for the analyst. He concludes that a transference pattern will be set up in therapy in which the therapist, because of her perceived power is designated as the external manifestation of the primitive harsh superego. When she refuses to take on this role in spite of repeated encouragement from the patient that she should do so, the situation arises in which she can begin to point out the difference between the scenario that the patient inhabits and the way in which the therapist is behaving in the present. Over time she lets examples accumulate of the way in which the patient perceives her and she puts together the tripartite interpretation which sets out:

- the past relationship that is being echoed
- the assumption made about the therapist
- the actual events in the present that contradict the belief.

In other words, the therapist initiates a campaign for evidence based living. Most therapists accept that evidence for their practice is importance and leads them to work in a relatively reliable and ethical way. My point here is that analytic therapy itself encourages an evidence based approach to life in which we are no longer content to see the world through the filters of our neurotic defences but constantly try to get closer to reality in all its sadness, savagery and beauty. She encourages the patient to test out the present but not to maintain a belief in the truths of the past when they are contrary to evidence about the present.

Transference to the Total Situation

Betty Joseph (1989) developed further the possible use of transference by her approach to the usefulness of transference when its meaning is broadened out. For many therapists, the only question asked is 'who am I for this patient?' A much more fruitful question is, as I have suggested above: 'To whom is this person talking?' Even that is a narrow focus on the individuals of the past and the present. Joseph described the relationship that was going on between her and her patient, N. He brought a dream in which he said 'there was a war going on'. This became the phrase that she used to think about the pattern of relating that he brought to her. There was always a war going on and it was much more useful to consider the way in which the ebb and flow of the session illustrated the nature of the war. On one occasion he was willing to agree that he understood what she was saying but that it did not help. From this point, she is able to use some specific images that he brings to enable him to see how the state of war was preventing him from using what was potentially positive and helpful in her. In other words, she moved from the total situation back to the individual and specific transference. This is much more likely to be helpful than sticking to the 'who am I now?' kind of question that beginners tend to ask themselves.

Tracing and using patterns in the clinical context is a process requiring great skill and humility. The therapist must be content often not to know the answers and to test carefully any hypothesis that she makes. There is no need for elaborate or complex formulations although an enigmatic intervention that is capable of various levels of meaning will be likely to set the patient wondering and testing the meaning for a long time in a way which can be very productive. On the other hand, the simpler an interpretation can be in its form, the more powerful it is likely to be. Above all it needs to be tied in closely to what the patient has just thought and experienced.

Conclusion

There are many ways of discovering and responding to a pattern of relating. The therapist will have her own difficulties in that she becomes a part of the system and will find herself reacting and acting both in her own feelings and sometimes in the nature of the interventions that she makes. This chapter has examined some of the ways in which theory, such as that developed by Melanie Klein, can help us to understand the complex nature of the interaction between patient and the receptive psyche of the therapist.

Discussion Points

Mr S came to see a male therapist after his male partner had left him to return to the United States. Mr S was devastated at being left and had indulged in a series of one off sexual encounters. The last one had ended at a bar with his partner getting involved in a fight. He says that he must change his lifestyle before he loses his job and/or gets seriously hurt. The therapist finds himself in each session feeling that he can understand the point that Mr S is making to him but when he says what he thinks, Mr S dismisses it scornfully and says that the therapist has not understood the depth of his feeling at all.

- What might be the required relationship here and what could the therapist possibly say about it?
- Take an intervention that you have made about a pattern of thinking and consider what made it more or less effective in your view.
- How could transference to the total situation help you to think about the recent sessions with one of your clients?
- How could the therapist's feelings have been used differently in the case of Mr J?

5 The Nature of the Evidence Base for Analytic Therapy

Questions to Consider While Reading

1. Why does the theory of human development matter to the therapist?
2. How can the patterns of physical development affect the mind of the adult?
3. What evidence can we have for the truth of psycho-analytic theory?

Introduction

So far, in support of the value of analysing patterns, this book has presented anecdotal evidence for the validity of the analytic model of human development that comes from within psychoanalytic practice through individual cases and from the inspiration of individual clinicians and thinkers. This chapter will look at the evidence base more closely. Language is of crucial importance to the development of the human adult and the human child gradually assumes her place in her society and her culture through a variety of steps, many of which involve a growing ability to use speech and writing. The young child is preoccupied with bodily functions and the demand of society that these functions should be controlled and relegated to a private space. These processes continue to dominate the individual after the process of the early stages has been negotiated.

Look at a newborn baby and ask yourself the question: how is this tiny, unspeaking, unseeing infant who can do nothing but breathe, cry, feed and excrete become the complex,

91

communicating, suffering adult that is now making the observation? If you have the good fortune to be able to observe a
baby from a position less closely involved than that of a parent,
you may be able to watch the amazing phenomenon of a baby
beginning not only to see but to look, not only looking but recognising and smiling, not only smiling but verbalising and so on
towards childhood. Most of this early process happens naturally
and, unless it is stopped by the absence of reinforcement and
encouragement. will continue to enable the individual to learn
to speak and to understand speech.

I once asked the zoologist Sir David Attenborough what he
thought was the defining quality of a human being as opposed
to an intelligent animal. His reply was that undoubtedly in his
mind, the defining quality is the ability to use language and communicate with each other in the nuanced detail that only human
language can provide. The human infant begins to be able to
recognise voices in the first few weeks and there is some evidence
to suggest that he recognises his mother's voice from before birth.
The dawning of conscious experience in those early weeks is one
of the most fascinating processes to watch.

But do we need to know what this early development
involves? The answer is that if you think that history and experience shape the human being but still allow for change, then
you must want to know what each individual might have gone
through and especially what he thinks he went through. Whatever that is, if it can be seen to affect the present, it can be an
important element in helping him to make his present free of the
limitations that the past could continue to impose.

If we want to know where the whole individual adult comes
from we need to know when and how the unconscious function
develops. Our need to understand the way in which the two systems of conscious process and unconscious process interact is the
reason for a developmental theory of the human mind. Is there
any connection apart from memory between what I thought
yesterday or ten years ago and what I think today? The world for
each one of us must begin with a kaleidoscope of discontinuous
and unorganised sensations.

Alan Schore, the neuro-scientist, asserts that the unconscious
is the first function to develop in the infant. The areas of the
brain that are associated with this development are primarily

in the right hemisphere. This area he says is the repository of the structures that mediate attachment and it constitutes what he calls our 'right mind'. According to the research evidence of the neuro-scientists, the human infant is able to use the right brain in the first year to develop structures that can be used to make affectional bonds with other people. In fact Schore states that the essential task of the first year is the

> Creation of a secure attachment bond between the infant and the primary caregiver. (003: 13)

If this is the case, the patterns that concern the psychological therapist are based on the structures that are established during the first year of life.

Developmental theory has been of monumental importance to therapy in the consulting room. We have moved a long way since Freud put forward the concept of *fixation*. In 1915 he published 'Instincts and their vicissitudes'. In it he put forward the importance of instincts or drives and emphasised that each instinct is satisfied through an object which is the 'thing' through which an instinct can achieve its satisfaction. Fixation occurs when an instinctive need or desire is satisfied either in reality or potentially through one part of the body or one other person and is not transferred to others as the individual grows and matures. This is the theory that underpins much psychoanalytic thinking. Even when thinking moved away from the emphasis on instincts and began to emphasise object relations, therapists have maintained an interest in the objects of desire that each person has chosen.

The Mouth

The theory of fixation implies that there is a developmental process that can be described and mapped. Each of the great thinkers in this field has held views on the essential landmarks in this mapping process. Freud focussed on the development of sexuality since in his view that was the basis of human mental and emotional functioning. The infant goes through well known stages represented by the prominence of one of the zones of the body.

The first stage is dominated by the mouth and its pleasures and pains. The newborn baby from the first hour can use its mouth to suck and, through that sucking, it appears to derive pleasure and satisfaction and we know as adults that it is a life giving process and the child must learn to suck efficiently in order to thrive.

As the weeks go by, the baby extends the pleasure to be had from the mouth on the nipple to take in other objects, usually his own fingers, fist, thumb or any part of the hand that can accidentally be brought near enough to be sucked. Some babies are given pacifiers or dummies and some are given bottles instead of the breast for various reasons. Whatever the substitute may be, the infant begins to recognise other objects but most babies to begin with will reject anything that does not provide milk. The experience of being given water is often met with disgust and anger so that the mouth may be the first area associated with pleasure, but also it may be the first area associated with frustration. Here may be the first negative patterns in the mental life of the individual.

There are of course adult physical experiences that echo the group of physical experiences connected with sucking. It is not difficult to see that smoking is one of these and all forms of idle sucking on pencils, pens and other objects may be reconnecting an adult with the lost pleasures of the baby. Sexuality can include oral pleasure or can focus entirely in this area which may or may not cause a problem for the adult. Mental functioning and its relationship to eating forms a vast and complex area with great potential for suffering for many people who are at risk of obesity or anorexia. The mental and emotional components of our relationships with food will include some patterns laid down for the small baby in his or her early days.

These are practical and bodily expressions of the remains of our attachment to the pleasures of the mouth. The adult who is in some sense repeating the infantile pattern of behaviour is likely to experience love in terms of the infant who is totally dependent on the primary care giver. The infant in this state makes demands that sound like matters of life and death. For the infant they were demands to keep him alive. The adult who is repeating patterns from this stage of life will feel helpless and will defend against the helplessness by whatever means he can find. Sometimes the defences will work and sometimes they will leave him even more helpless as well as frustrated. The adult who falls in love while this pattern still strongly affects him will feel love as a desire to consume to ingest and to take entirely into himself the other person. He will have the accompanying anxieties of emptying and exhausting the other.

> Mr J came to a therapist because his wife of five years had walked out taking his three year old son with her. He said that she was very moody at times and he knew that he had not always been considerate of how she might have felt. He thought that he could not live without her but that she would never want to return to him. In fact he thought that she had probably already found someone else because, although she denied that there was another man, he had driven past the house and seen a strange car parked outside. He was full of expressions of apology to the therapist: 'you will find me boring; I know I just go on and on about the same thing; you will see why she couldn't put up with me'.

Mr J gradually unfolded to the therapist the story of his short marriage. He had met his wife Alice through his friend's girl-friend. She had been a work colleague and was in his words 'beautiful and intelligent and everything I could have wanted'. He had felt that he must possess her and had made a great effort to impress her with flowers, gifts, cards and a not altogether truthful account of his own success and prowess in his work. She had responded to his onslaught but he suspected that she had already formed a relationship with another colleague of his at work. He had confronted his colleague and demanded that he leave Alice alone. The colleague had denied that he had anything more than a friendship but Mr J had never believed him and had suffered agonies of jealousy refusing to go on holiday or out dancing in case Alice would 'meet someone better than me'.

All this amounted to a most painful account of oral jealousy. Mr J wanted to own his woman as many lovers would, but his demand for sole ownership was tainted with painful jealousy which can be observed in the infant who wants and claims sole ownership of the breast.

Mr J has also taken his jealousy to the next stage which Klein describes when the infant in phantasy drinks the milk and leaves the breast empty and unable to satisfy him again. Klein called images like this 'unconscious phantasy' to distinguish it from conscious fantasy or day dreaming. In other words, a pattern of feeling and responding was established at the earliest stage of development which was repeated and projected onto new situations where intense emotion was experienced. Mr J, in Klein's terms, was re-experiencing his need to have the food that his mother could give him and to be secure that he could have it when he needed it. To be secure, it is best to own the source of supply as most adults realise. Even this would not solve his problems though because in his own mind, the source of supply, in this case his wife Alice, was harmed and damaged by his need and not able to be available or useful to him because of his own actions. This is perhaps an adult description of what Klein saw as an infantile experience. It is a way of redescribing in theoretical terms the problem that Mr J brings. Does such a theoretical approach help us to know how to help Mr J?

Oral Patterns in Therapy

The therapist here would need to be careful in working with this kind of experience. The patient, Mr J, is an adult man and in working with a female therapist is likely to experience the helplessness and humiliation of a small boy with his mother as well as a parallel experience to that with his wife in which he feels useless and damaging. The therapist has to deal both with the danger that anything she says that is right could add to his sense of inadequacy and also that she can intensify his masochism if she makes him think that she sees him as a baby. The therapist will try to concentrate on helping to articulate the intensity of his feeling. This will be difficult and dangerous if he is at all suicidal. The degree of potential for suicidal ideation or intention should always be established at the beginning of the work in so far as the patient is able or willing to say what he feels. At least the therapist has to seek to know how close he is to destroying the part of himself that he hates and despises. She needs to help him to see that this is not the whole of himself and that there is another part of him too. In the case of Mr J she already knows that he has been successful in his work since he boasted about it to his wife. He now thinks that such boasting was pathetic and that he had nothing really to boast about. This complete turnaround may be challenged because he may be using it as a way to preserve his image of Alice as being infinitely superior to him. Like the knights in the narratives of the period of chivalry, he has an impulse to keep the lady good, pure and infinitely better than he is so that she can be worshipped as the good part of mother who could give to her baby if she chose to do so even though he was so unworthy. If he can believe in her goodness, virtue and distance from him, she may still be available to him and unspoilt by his own unworthiness and greed.

Things Go In and Things Come Out

Janine Sternberg collected in 2005 some of her current thinking on the rationale for including an observational study of the human infant in training for psychotherapists and psychoanalysts. She has carried out some careful observational research which she reports and she develops some thinking about the benefits for therapist trainees in training of seeing for themselves the way in which the human infant becomes a social, relating, communicating being. The process affects the trainee in training at a profound level (2005: 84). The process has strong ethical requirements and demands skill and sensitivity from the observer but, if well done, can be a support and encouragement for the mother who may appreciate the interest that is being shown in her and her baby. Sternberg uses the image of music to convey what must be played delicately and with respect. The observer's interest, of course, must never under normal circumstances extend to interference in the process.

One of the reasons for asking trainees in analytic training to observe a mother and baby is to give them an opportunity to see for themselves whether there is validity in a developmental theory of the human mind as well as the human body. Thinking based on stages of development implies at least three phases in which the adult's functioning may be focussed. After the oral stage comes the anal. In other words, the baby takes in through his mouth and then has to excrete. The one follows the other and both are needed for the infant to feel comfortable and at ease. Feeding is not always comfortable but is more likely to be comfortable than excretion which leads to a cold or sticky sensation after the initial relief. It also leads to a more ambivalent relationship with caregivers who may express disgust or at least distaste and will be startled and often angry if the baby urinates on the unprotected lap. The baby sometimes appears to take immense enjoyment and pleasure in the nappy changing process when the mother or care giver may be sufficiently relaxed to play with the baby, tickling, caressing and smiling. The baby in response may smile and enter into a reciprocal affective exchange which is very important in developing the baby's brain and his ability to relate.

Socialisation and Language

As the infant grows, the expectation that he will learn to control his sphincter and bowel and will not need nappies will begin to affect his relationship with his important adults. Cultural practices vary and within cultures there are wide variations in the methods used to train children to use the lavatory and the degree of tolerance of his mistakes. The unconscious patterns that may be laid down at this stage will usually relate to control and restraint. The adults will reflect back an image of approval or disapproval that is increasingly strong as the child begins to be mobile and to be capable of creating all sorts of additional problems for the adults. One of the best known examples of popular psychoanalysis is the idea of the 'anal personality' who is inclined to gather and keep things to himself; whether the things are stamps or the names of species of birds. Collecting and being proud of one's collection can be seen as the adult version of the toddler's pride in his faeces which his mother will praise him for collecting into the appropriate place. Little girls are similarly affected by praise and blame but are not so likely to receive it from their fathers and therefore the process may lack something of the excitement that it holds for boys.

Mr X had some qualities that might be thought to relate to this stage of development:

Mr X came to see a therapist because his ex wife wanted to deny him access to his little boy aged three. He was very attached to his child but was furiously angry with his ex wife whom he accused of all sorts of neglect and unworthiness. He said in the initial consultation that he hoped to be helped to become more able to help his little boy and the therapist suspected, also to be more impressive to the courts about his suitability to have access. He was a large man who worked in a care home for older people and was full of the hardships that life had imposed on him. He began the early sessions by saying 'It's happened again.' What had happened again was that someone or something had disappointed him or let him down in some way. He had taken his car for a service and was charged a large sum for various repairs. He then found that the fan belt needed replacing. He had to take the car back and this made him miss an important appointment. So no matter how hard he tries, he says that he can't get anything to work for him.

Much of the material that Mr X brought to therapy related to cleanliness and hygiene. He complained that his wife did not keep his little boy clean enough and he often spoke of the conditions in the care home where he worked as being dirty. It was not well enough looked after in various ways. He also spoke of a dream in which he was floating in the sky like the boy in the film of 'The Snowman'. He came down to look at Earth and found himself shitting on the village where he had lived as a child. He was very ashamed of this part of the dream and had great difficulty in telling his female therapist about it. He said that the first part of the dream was wonderfully exhilarating. He did not say that the last part was not and his therapist said that perhaps the whole thing was exhilarating but that it would be difficult to acknowledge this even to himself. He agreed.

This man had found marriage and fatherhood both 'wonderful' and yet in some way also shameful and humiliating. He responded to the humiliation of being seen by his wife and his son by becoming extremely fussy about details and especially about cleanliness. He had driven his wife away partly by what she freely called his 'obsessionality'. He was an adult who seemed to be repeating the patterns that he had learned from his depressed and demanding mother. He could not please her enough to get her to lift him out of his cot and be hugged with love and acceptance. He had formed unconscious theories about why he was not wanted by her or by his father. His therapist was able to work with his anal difficulties because he also felt that she would not want to hear about his shitty, smelly fantasies. His unconscious phantasies of his unworthiness were even more of a problem until she helped him to come to some understanding of what he was still trying to do and how inappropriate that was in his present adult state.

Language Leads Forward

By the time the infant is walking and achieving control of his bladder and bowel he has already achieved language and conscious thoughts and images. Linguistic philosophers and historians attest the amazing achievement of the human infant in learning to speak and hear. Language gives an opportunity to begin to think about one's own mental functioning. It also sets us at a distance from the things that we can name. They can be referred to instead of touched or felt. If we accept the concept of an unconscious function, we might expect that it would begin to affect thinking and feeling. In some ways it is easier for us to think of the child having a mass of unconscious patterns or structures than it is to see how the conscious mind develops. In fact, consciousness is one of the great remaining puzzles. What is it and how does it function? Susan Greenfield has written a very clear layman's guide to the *Human Brain* (Greenfield, 1997). The science moves and changes quickly and the layman cannot easily keep up with new thinking. The question of memory, what it is and how it functions is raised as soon as we begin to think of consciousness as a condition of being human. Only by being conscious and able to reflect on one's self and one's environment could mankind have reached the age of tools and co-operation, let alone the age of technology in which we live. The study of consciousness and its component memories has always been difficult because the main instrument for studying it is consciousness itself. We know it primarily from first person experience but we cannot get outside the function that we are trying to study.

What Do We Really Know About the Development of Consciousness?

Neuro-science has transformed the possibilities for understanding the connection between mind and brain. While paying attention to Polly Young-Eisendrath's warning of the dangers of *biobabble* or a 'knee-jerk biological determinism' (2001: 201), we cannot and should not ignore the ways in which the biologists have been helping psychoanalysis to clarify and validate its position. The reaction against the perceived reductionism of the biologists has been fierce in those who would sympathise with Young Eisendrath's dismissal of it all as *biobabble*. While remembering that we are interested in subjectivity and the individual, we also can make more sense of ourselves by considering findings about the biological base of mind. Understanding the ways in which neurology and biology can be related to mind is still evolving. Francis Scalzone (2005) writes of relationships suggesting that the validation of psychoanalysis is not a good enough reason to turn to neuro-science although he does make clear that he can see connections:

> In many neurological syndromes there is a concomitant psychic disturbance which suggests that a relationship exists between the neuropathology and the psychopathology although the psychic symptoms cannot be related to organic lesion because the psychic functions do not reside in the neuroanatomical structures... (2005: 1408)

One of the links proposed by Scalzone is in the learning process of imitation. He quotes Gallese who writes of 'imitating in order to perceive and then imitating in order to know' (ibid: 1416). This is an area of neuro-science that is clearly relevant to the understanding of transference. If imitation can be shown to have a biological base in the way that the human organism learns to function in its environment, then we have better grounds for saying that the patterns acquired by the infant and the child will be important in later life and will need to be carefully analysed in order to be changed. If the baby and child learn by imitating, the adult may learn from the model of the therapist who can contain her anxiety, manage her fears and make her anger into something constructive. Above all, she models the ability to think about distressing experience rather than just reacting to it.

We have in fact some reliable information about the development of infant consciousness. There is much more to learn but we have good reason to think that babies and children are changed by their experiences and that genetics, environment and psychology interact to shape the way in which the experience is used throughout life. In spite of the difficulties and the differences between scientific method and the methods of psychoanalytic research, there is now the possibility of a science of consciousness, which will not supersede the experience of the individual but will complement an anecdotal account of analysis. The human baby can be seen from many different angles. Sue Gerhardt, writing for a broadly popular audience of parents and therapists, rejects Freud's biologically determined baby:

> ... it does not satisfy my own sense of the way the body and mind develop because it proposes a much more self made and self generated individual than I believe to be the case ... For example the poorly handled baby develops a more reactive stress response and different biochemical patterns from a well handled baby. The brain itself is a social organ ... (2004: 14)

The idea that our early affective experiences will influence the future not only through memory, but through biochemical traces is now well accepted and has become part of popular culture. We now have techniques to study brain function and very slowly understanding is emerging that mind can be mapped onto brain function which itself can be studied. Antonio Dimasio wrote in 2000:

> Over the past two decades, work in cognitive neuroscience has become especially rewarding because the development of new techniques to observe the brain in terms of its structure and function now permits us to link a certain behaviour we observe clinically or in an experiment, not only to the presumed mental counterpart of that behaviour but also to specific indices of brain structure or brain activity. (2000: 13)

Does the Brain Itself Matter to Therapists?

Many psychotherapists have asked why they should be interested in the brain. If someone is suspected of having a brain dysfunction we would send them to their physician. In the capacity of psychotherapist, we would not expect to be able to diagnose or treat such a disorder. There are some well recognised possible symptoms such as fainting, severe headaches, fits and visual disturbance but they can all indicate other conditions and there are many other possible symptoms depending on the area of pressure. In my view it is wise for the main symptoms of a tumour or other major brain disease to be taught in all training courses so that the danger signals such as unusual headaches, blurred or double vision in the case of a possible tumour can be recognised and the appropriate referral can be made. A recommendation that the patient should seek a medical assessment is the wise and ethical step for a non-medically trained psychotherapist to take in such a case. Our task is primarily to understand the psychological component of behaviour in the present. On the other hand, those who work with children or adolescents need to understand something of normal development in order to make use of a concept such as transference, which implies that something unnecessary is happening: the anxiety or the depression is greater than the external circumstances combined with the state of the organism would normally allow. Each practitioner therefore needs to understand enough developmental biology to recognise something that is out of the developmental path for the individual. If the neuro-scientists and biologists can help us to distinguish a transferred emotional reaction which is out of place for a particular person in a particular situation from a normal developmental stage, they can assist the therapeutic process. In general terms we can look at the developmental stage and in particular terms we can look at what troubles the individual patient. Such an understanding opens the way for a study of the ability to transfer learning from the past. Not being able to do so will limit the ability to move to new relationships and will prevent a person from understanding his world and therefore responding confidently to those around him. The ability to make a transference is an essential quality of humanity.

While a psychotherapist needs to be able to discern when there is a physical implication and the patient may need the help of the medical practitioner, she also needs to be able to work with the patient who is somatising a psychological phenomenon which cannot yet be thought about. This is entirely within the province of the psychological practitioner but is by no means easy as Peter Shoenberg (2007) points out. The patient may have been for a battery of tests to discover the cause and cure for a physical condition

> Often the patient will arrive rather passively, feeling already rejected by their referring doctor with whom they may have had a significant long-term relationship.   (2007: 26)

He emphasises the part played by resistance for such a patient and that there will also be considerable anxiety for the therapist who will still worry about whether the physical symptoms are life threatening or in need of the treatment that the patient so earnestly and probably omnipotently desires. In fact, one of the most difficult parts of the assessment and initial work with such a patient is the movement to a psychological approach that will bring to an end the hope of a physical cure and the secondary gains from the symptoms. Many such patients cling with great tenacity to the view that they have a physical illness and that the doctors have just not found the truth yet. Such a patient will be extremely resistant to any analytic work and especially to any interpretations which gets too near to the truth:

> Mrs J came to see a therapist because the General Practitioner physician could find no physical cause for her exhaustion and continuous headaches. She thought that he had not sent her for all the possible tests and was most unwilling to see the psychotherapist. In fact, she said that she had only come in order to show that this would not help so that she could get on with the tests that the doctor was denying her. The therapist listened quietly and said that perhaps it would be a help to her if her physical problems could be helped by psychotherapy even though that might be slower and would certainly demand more from her. He took care to speak always of the symptoms as something that he accepted as genuinely experienced.

After several sessions she began to acknowledge the anger that she felt with her husband and the jealousy of his mother with whom he had a very close relationship. She began to say that perhaps her illness which was still totally physical to her might help her to show him that she had needs too. In fact she began to see that it was counter productive for her because he simply brought this mother round to help in the house. When she had said this, she began the long slow process of finding out what else has contributed to this way of expressing her protest.

Transference as Attachment

The establishment of the areas of the brain function that will enable the infant to form attachments to others and to become aware of his own existence as an entity, both like and unlike others, develops after birth:

> Over the course of the first year limbic circuitries emerge in a sequential progression from amygdala to anterior cingulate to insula and finally to orbitofrontal... And so as a result of attachment experiences, this system enters a critical period of maturation in the last quarter of the first year, the same time that working models of attachment are first measured. (Schore 2003: 19)

The capacity for attachment coincides with the acquisition of a lexicon of affects and the ability to recognise them in human non-verbal behaviour, particularly in the face. This ability, that is crucial to empathy of any sort, is also essential in the development of the ability to form a transference. Schore quotes Adolphs et al.: 'recognising emotions from visually presented facial expressions requires right somato-sensory representations that stimulate how the individual would feel when displaying a certain facial expression' (2003: 23). When this process takes place, the individual is able to predict behaviour from non-verbal prompts but a large part of the processing involved takes place outside of consciousness.

This conclusion is of great importance because it assures us that the emotional experience of transference situations is not just an enactment of some aspects of what has happened before. It is actually a reworking of the emotional experience. This enables us to see why the experiences in therapy may be as vivid as the original experience and as painful or as joyful as the experience that has now been forgotten or repressed. Bringing the original memory to consciousness, if that can be done, has to cause a repetition of the original emotions but of course if that happens we must also allow for those emotional traces to be overwritten with the new experience.

What Does the Transference from Infancy Tell Us?

These conclusions from the neuro-scientists give some help to psychotherapists in establishing a relationship in which transference can take place and can show itself. The human baby has emotional experiences of great depth and intensity connected with feeding, warmth, safety and all the care that make him feel safe and comfortable. Gradually these experiences form memory traces which coalesce in a feeling of love associated with a few other human beings, usually the immediate family. The component parts of the feelings of love will often lose their separate identity in consciousness although the memory of those component experiences will be stored in the *lexicon of affects*. Although these experiences may not always be available to conscious recall they will be available through the connections in the orbitocortical system to the formation of responses in the future.

Such a view of the relationship between short and vivid immediate experiences and the longer term ongoing self structure is expressed in Betty Joseph's paper on 'Transference; the total situation' (1989) (see Chapter 4). In this paper she describes the concept of transference as a structure in relationship and therefore it has a continuing existence while the immediate, brief experiences flicker into life and die away again:

> My stress will be on the idea of transference as a framework in which something is always going on, where there is always movement and activity. (1989: 156)

Making explicit this broad view of transference enabled Joseph to see the importance of carrying the investigations well beyond the specifics of the relationship to the analyst. Everything that happens including the reminiscences about other people and the 'atmosphere' that he builds up enables the analyst to understand some communication from the patient about his past. (ibid.)

The Third Stage

The small child who, by the age of two or three is walking, speaking, eating the same food as adults and in many ways behaving like an adult human being still has major psychological development in front of him if he is to become a functioning adult. He has to learn to make a loving sexual relationship. He begins according to the Freudian narrative by observing his parents. Freud wrote about the nuclear family that he saw, including servants and nannies who were often for the children more important than parents. We can see many different family structures in the twenty first century. The template situation for the child in Western Europe in the twentieth century was a nuclear family with a mother, father (preferably the biological father), a child and siblings. Grandparents may be somewhere around but may not play a major role. Often this template is not what any given child can expect. In addition multi-cultural societies lead to many different expectations of what is desirable for the growing child.

The psychotherapist who wishes to enable the patient to demonstrate these remnants of the early affective experiences will need to create an environment which is as much as possible like the original situation for the infant. She will recreate a setting in which there is a dependency and a need to trust the powerful figure who can make life safe or not, comfortable or not and in the longer term can be loved in whatever way the individual is capable of loving. This might be considered to lend weight to the analytic technique of asking the patient to lie down on a couch. Freud asked his patients to lie down because he did not wish them to be looking at him all day long. The prone position in relation to the seated analyst obviously does also lead to a greater likelihood of regression to a state of infantile dependency. For those who have not experienced this position for themselves, this statement may seem to imply a risk of iatrogenic dysfunction, or a problem caused by the treatment itself. For anyone who has lain on a psychotherapist's or psychoanalyst's couch, there can be little doubt that it encourages regression and increases the responsibility of the therapist. Even when he is in a seated position, the patient's transference from early infantile states can be observed so that we do not have to assume that the regression is caused only or exclusively by lying on the couch.

On the other hand, the therapist's awareness of the importance for the newborn baby of the mother's face implies a need for eye contact at least for some people at the beginning. The newborn shows such interest in the human face in preference to other shapes from the point where she is able to look and focus her eyes that we have to acknowledge that lack of the possibility of eye contact may be an important deprivation. The mother's eye is the main focus of communication between the mother and her baby. What does the therapist do therefore if she encourages the use of the couch and the patient is deprived of the looking into each other's eyes that has such a powerful developmental potential for the infant? One effect is to hold the patient in the state which is clearly a regression from the state of adulthood which he occupies. The frustration of not seeing the therapist throws him back on his own resources and makes sure that he cannot become too dependent. A degree of useful dependence can be achieved for the patient with the help of the experienced, well trained therapist but without specific training should not be risked.

So why should we even consider this risky procedure? We can now reasonably expect that conditions that echo infancy or perhaps emphasise its frustrations will also encourage the use of those areas of the brain that are involved in recognising the experiences of infancy. When these areas of the brain are stimulated by a new experience of the recognised affect, they are also susceptible to receiving new terms that can be added to the vocabulary. We are not just wiping out some of the past and adding new. We may also be able to modify some of the terms that already exist so that the experience of a certain tone of voice or facial expression may become a minor irritation rather than an impending catastrophe.

Creating a Continuous Sense of Self

Antonio Dimasio (2000) defines consciousness in various ways, one of which leads to other conclusions:

> Consciousness depends on the internal construction and exhibition of new knowledge concerning an interaction between that organism and an object. (2000: 169)

There is a relationship between the sensori-motor map that is created by a perception in the brain and the organism's response to the map that it creates. Thus the experience of a particular sound will make a difference to the whole map:

> As the images of the object affect the state of the organism, yet another level of brain structure creates a swift non-verbal account of the events that are taking place in the varied brain regions activated as a consequence of the object-organism interaction. The mapping of the object related consequences occurs in first-order neural maps representing proto self and object. (2000: 170)

Dimasio goes on to say that the nonverbal account narrates a story and that it is in this process of narration that the story teller begins to exist.

We therefore have the valuable insight that the process of forming an attachment to the psychotherapist will in itself be composed of many affective episodes. The mere creation of the unconscious narratives that these episodes form together will enable the individual to begin to form a more useful sense of self. In other words, the process of affective experience that goes on in therapy is a process which enables self recognition and is also a process which enables transference recognition in the future. It does not matter whether the object being perceived by the brain is in the present or is a memory from the past. Core consciousness is composed of both and both will be capable of allowing the organism to be aware of itself as the perceiver or knower and therefore as a self.

This core self, created out of images in the brain, is essentially transitory, forever created and forever lost. Dimasio quotes T.S. Eliot: 'You are the music while the music lasts' (2000: 172). We would have problems in continuity if this were the sum total of brain activity. More stable and more developmentally long term is what has generally become known as 'the autobiographical self'. This is an aggregate of the records of the individual experiences stored in the right brain. These records will consist of some permanent facts such as my name, what I consider to be the essential elements of my identity, historical and consistent facts which are only slightly subject to modification by later experiences and the elements that can be changed by experience. Hence 'The display of autobiographical self is thus more open to refashioning than the core self which is reproduced time and again in essentially the same form across a lifetime' (2000: 173). Nevertheless, the autobiographical self, which will feel like the central self to most of us, is dependent for its existence on the continued renewal of the transient core consciousness. During a loss of core consciousness as in an epileptic fit, there is no possibility of an autobiographical self.

Transference is not Merely a Memory

Dimasio also helps us to understand why the experiences recreated in transference during a therapeutic experience are so vivid. They are recalled as elements for the unconscious store and they bring with them aspects of the organism's motor involvement in the original process of perception. This adds to the force of the new process that is evoked in therapy and means that the emotion is not merely a memory. Since the right hemisphere of the brain is the place where early affective experiences are processed and stored, it is the right brain that deals with these processes of affect regulation and recognition, much of which is unconscious. The right brain is also the repository of the memory of affect-laden experiences according to Schore (2003: 24).

Neuropsychological studies now also reveal that the right hemisphere, 'the right mind', and not the later forming verbal-linguistic left is the substrate of affectively laden autobiographical memory. (2003: 24)

This statement is clearly of major importance in understanding the processes that might be involved in transference. The actual memory that is being transferred is part of a lexicon of indicators of affect and will also have connections to personal autobiographical memories of affective experiences. We now can see that the work of the neuro-scientists is enabling us to see how the two requirements for thinking: memory and perception, are in fact connected in the processing carried out by the brain as well as in its outcome. We can now see more clearly that transference involves an unconscious process in which the stimulus of recognising a cue to an affective response in another is taken in at an unconscious level but although it is unconscious it can stimulate the affect recognition centres in the brain of the subject. In other words when I meet a stranger who stimulates a memory that is now unconscious, I will have the same responses in my affect and behaviour in the present as I did when I first encountered the experiences.

Ms J came to see a therapist because she was undertaking social work training and was finding that the rest of the training group were inexplicably hostile to her. She said that she was sure she did nothing to annoy them but no-one seemed to want to go and have coffee with her after the seminars. She seemed pleasant and willing to co-operate with the therapist who was at a loss to know what might be the matter. In the third session she described an experience in which she had told the group leader that she really admired him and thought that he could be more helpful to her if he would only notice what she was going though. She said 'I don't know what came over me to say that in front of everyone. I suppose you'll say it had something to do with my father.' The therapist knew very little about her father and had no such intention but waited hopefully. 'My father would just stand and watch while my two older sisters teased me until I cried. Then one day I managed to get him to tell them off for being so mean. I think

I have been hoping that he would tell the group off and maybe I have thought I needed help when I could have talked to them myself.'

This sort of insight came after other transference work in which the therapist had been able to be helpful so that Ms J was beginning to have an autobiographical self which could be thought about and understood.

Do We Preserve the Negative Patterns More than the Positive?

There is one other aspect of the study of the formation of the affect lexicon that is particularly relevant to the formation of transference. This is an argument that can be traced from Freud through object relations theorists and is also validated by the work of neuro-scientists such as Alan Schore. Following one of Freud's main themes, Schore set out in several papers his view of the way in which we deal with reality. For example, he wrote of the way in which we all begin with trying to maximise pleasure and minimise unpleasure. This he, like Freud, called the pleasure principle. Childhood presents a process in which we have to learn to face reality which cannot be totally shut out even by neurotic defences. Adult life, according to Freud demands that we try to live by the reality principle:

> The replacement of the pleasure principle by the reality principle, with all the psychical consequences involved which is here schematically condensed into one sentence is not in fact accomplished all at once. (1925: 39)

The search for pleasure can be seen as the central driving motivation in human behaviour. With this motivation, the human mind is able to respond by alertness to unpleasant experience. If this is the chief meta motivation of human nature, psychoanalysis had to elaborate what it might mean in the mind of individuals. Theory has to encompass the ways in which we can assimilate experience so that the child and later the adult will repress what is unpleasant but will still be able to make use of them to help him to avoid similar situations in the future. For this reason, W.R.D. Fairbairn (1952) argues that only the bad object is internalised. The organism has no need to control the good object and will therefore not need to internalise it. In object relations terms, he is describing the motivation for storing the experiences which will constitute negative transference rather than those that will build up a dictionary of pleasant experiences.

Fairbairn's (1952) view of the process of developing the psyche is also important in terms of the reason why transference is needed. The child and the adult after him need to be able to control the bad and frightening experiences so that they will not threaten him. He cannot be sure that he will be able to do this but he can take an impression of the cues that will warn him. Since the storage of these cues is not a matter of conscious or deliberate recall, the system will work under stress or when the organism is not particularly on guard. One might argue that in the therapeutic situation the system is always on guard. Most people enter a therapeutic relationship with all sorts of anxiety and caution. A (female) friend is just describing her first therapy:

'I chose a woman because I had heard about this business of transference and I did not want to fall in love with my therapist'.

She is older and wiser now although in fact she did not fall in love with her first woman therapist. She tells me that she was quite unmoved by her:

'She was very formal and there was no question of anything but a professional relationship with her. I knew I would never feel any affection for her but I thought that I might be able to remember something more useful. I asked her whether I should lie down on the couch because I thought that more should happen.'

My friend became aware that actually she was disappointed that she did not feel like falling in love with this rather stiff and very proper therapist. She is not at all a reserved or unemotional person and I would have expected her to be able to demonstrate her ability to love very readily. What she was demonstrating however, was the pattern of caution that she had learned as a child. Her father was a stiff and proper paterfamilias who would not allow his children to bother him when he wanted to read the paper or read a book. As a result, the implicit memory laid down in the right brain has an effect now when there is a question of love even though the question itself was in this case unconscious. My friend had convinced herself that she could relax and not need to be on guard but her unconscious lexicon still looked up the signals and produced the cautions that had been necessary in the past.

The neuro-scientist can therefore offer help to the therapist both in validating what we learn empirically from our work and by giving shape to the biological substrate that both forms the limits and shows the places where change will be possible in the complex organism that we recognise as the mind. Mind is much more than the sum of the parts of the brain but it cannot exist without brain. Just as mind is based in brain, psychoanalysis is based in evidence that is ultimately derived from our knowledge of the human body. As this chapter has shown, the development of the body enables and requires a parallel development of the mind. The therapist needs to have an eye and an ear for both.

Conclusion

This chapter has argued that there are patterns in human development that are sufficiently general to provide a useful level of expectation. Some of the patterns are essential to survival. For example a baby who does not know that her mouth is important is unlikely to thrive. The adult who has not moved beyond that emphasis and put the desires associated with the mouth into context and under constraint will experience difficulties in relationships and may show addictive behaviour. On the other hand identifying transference is not a simple matter of x = y. What is transferred can appear in a disguised form or can appear in the form of transference to a total situation. This is a valuable concept that can help the therapist to locate the nature of a pattern that she is experiencing with a patient and formulate a useful response.

Discussion Points

1. Consider Ms J on p. 111:

    'My father would just stand and watch while my two older sisters teased me until I cried. Then one day I managed to get him to tell them off for being so mean. I think I have been hoping that he would tell the group off and maybe I have thought I needed help when I could have talked to them myself.'

    What might the therapist say, if anything, to Ms J at this point?
2. Why should an analytic practitioner be interested in the development of the infant?
3. What might you lose if you practise analytic therapy without knowing anything about the brain?
4. Why might the oral stage leave the adult with a feeling of guilt he cannot account for?

6 How Much Can We Achieve Through Analysing Transference Patterns?

Questions to Consider While Reading:

1. How much can analytic work achieve and what are its limitations?
2. What is a transference cure?
3. Why do some patients not change?
4. What is a corrective emotional experience?

Introduction

So far, this book has set out to show that various kinds of transference patterns have a theoretical justification and that they are clinically useful. But just how clinically useful can they be? We have been told by writers such as David Malan (1995) that understanding the origin of a problem and the reasons for its power over the patient in the present, may still not be enough to enable the patient to change. We reach a point with some people where they will say to the therapist 'I understand all that now but I still don't know what to do about it.' The question that may then have to be considered is whether it is helpful to let the therapy continue when it is not clear that it can bring about any further useful change. Patients come to see us not just to have an interesting experience or an intellectual stimulus. They come in order to feel better, happier and to lead more satisfying lives. We never, as Marion Milner put it, promised them a rose garden but that is what they expect. The most careful explanation of the nature and limitations of analytic work given verbally or in writing can still be largely unheard by the person who is longing for solutions and to be made better. This chapter will therefore take the question that most bothers therapists: how much can we achieve through analytic work?

What is a Cure?

The word *cure* is linked to the notions of both the removal of symptoms of an illness and also to pastoral care. The Latin word *cura* implied both meanings and the pastoral meaning survives in the religious office of *curate* and the task of that office which is the *cure of souls*.

When it comes to a physical illness we might think that we are usually fairly clear about what *cure* might mean. If I have a cough, I am cured when I am no longer coughing. On further examination, even that is not totally clear. I might consider myself cured if I still cough occasionally but am not distressed by it and do not bother other people to the extent that they would complain about my coughing. Generally, people speak about feeling 'better' but do not always mean it in a relative sense. All of this tends to show that 'cure' is psychological. If I feel that I am well, I am well. *Cure* or the lack of it is demonstrated over time, and many patients will reserve judgment when therapy ends. The client might well at that point be aware that moods change and he may become depressed again. For this reason many people ask whether they may return to therapy in the future if they feel the need and are not sure enough of their 'betterness' to walk away.

People consult with a therapist because they are in distress. They have some idea of what is the matter but the reasons for the distress may be hidden in the unconscious. The therapist may arrive at a formulation that differs considerably from that of the patient. The ethical problem that this can cause is discussed in Chapter 7. Sometimes a whole therapy is spent in trying to find out what the patient needs and what his desire could be. A Lacanian view following Freud's emphasis on the importance of hidden wishes would lead a therapist to help a patient to search for the truth of his own desire and to recognise how that is different from the desire of his mother or another which he will have taken on. An object relations therapist would also seek to help the patient to find his true desire and in finding it to find his ability to relate to his own good objects and to deal with his frightening negative feelings or objects so that he can allow them to co-exist. Therapists of most disciplines will seek to help the patient to find his own truth and the courage to acknowledge it so that he can find a way of living with it without needing to resort to neurotic symptoms.

Of course it is possible to administer questionnaires and some clinical services will routinely seek to discover the base line for the therapeutic work. There are well established research instruments to measure levels of depression and anxiety at the beginning of therapy. This sort of careful measure enables therapists to measure change and symptom improvement. It risks the emphasis on symptoms that has led to the success of cognitive forms of therapy at the expense of analytic work. Clinical services such as that of **WPF** Therapy use the Clinical Outcomes Routine Evaluation (CORE) framework to evaluate their work and will administer questionnaires (including the relevant questionnaires as well as service delivery evaluation questionnaires). Other individuals may choose to participate in research studies or evaluation of outcomes but will not usually choose to use questionnaires as a tool to discover what their patient needs or wishes to achieve. The first assessment interview session will reveal far more than most questionnaires about what is going on beneath the surface. The facts that can be contained in the answers to a questionnaire might be useful complements to this, giving background information but will not be enough for the analytic therapist. If you ask questions, all you get are answers. The analytic therapist needs much more from the patient than answers to questions which by being asked have set an agenda and determined the direction of the patient's thinking.

Patients will be able to tell you what they consciously know, and sometimes they may be willing to write down a great deal. Like their spoken words, the patients' written words will convey a surface message but deeper knowledge will remain hidden unless, and until, the analytic work can enable it to appear. We begin with the conscious problems that are known and already have words. In my book on beginning the therapy I examined the way in which the initial session can establish transference patterns for the therapy (Murdin 2005). Once he knows this he is already likely to be much better. On the other hand, some problems are clear and manifest and both patient and therapist might acknowledge that disabling symptoms such as depression need attention.

In analytic work in the twenty first century the symptoms brought at the beginning are not usually the physical symptoms that were brought to psychoanalysis in the early days and are still occasionally brought to a therapist or a psychiatrist, such as hysterical paralysis, severe obsessions or delusions but are the often the more diffuse forms of unhappiness. Presenting problems brought to **WPF** Therapy which sees a range of clients for psychoanalytic psychotherapy and for once weekly psychodynamic counselling for most frequently depression, followed by relationship and work difficulties. Depression can be measured on various scales and improvements can be measured both by self reporting and by research instruments. The analytic therapists who do not administer questionnaires content themselves with helping their patients to understand their own symptoms and give verbal expression to what the body might have been both concealing and demonstrating. This is one of the reasons why there are great difficulties in measuring the outcomes of analytic work.

When researchers have examined specific problems such as bereavement, they have found good outcomes for counselling therapy. Taking the conscious needs of clients such as the pain of bereavement, Roth and Fonagy (2008: 258) cite a 1977 study of 200 bereaved women who were offered counselling based on psychodynamic exploratory methods for three months. At follow up, 77 per cent of the counselled group had good outcomes contrasted with 41 per cent of controls. This sort of result is useful in convincing government and statutory agencies of the importance of psychodynamic, analytic therapies but it also shows how necessary to research is a defined presenting problem. Where they can be defined, they help us to measure outcomes but they may be only a small part of the story for the therapy if it is allowed to explore the patient's needs at length and in depth.

Patients are often quite definite in their views of what they are looking for as a cure when they are still quite near the beginning of their therapy. They can say that the therapy is helpful or that it is completely useless. A lengthy and profound analysis is less clear cut. The effects of a thorough analysis of the unconscious elements in the patient's mental functioning will lead to some further suffering during the process but will also lead to a general sense of being more in control of one's mental state through being able to think about it constructively. This process of change can be described in specific theoretical terms by each variation of the models of analytic therapy. The following box sums up some of the ways in which analytical therapists might conceive of their aims:

- Achieving the depressive position (tolerating good and bad, ambivalence, guilt and reparation)
- Achieving a capacity for concern
- Achieving a sense of continuity of the self in time
- Achieving a resolution of transference neurosis
- Achieving the transcendent function and tolerating the existence of opposites
- Achieving the ability to reflect on experience
- Achieving the ability to use language to symbolise experience
- Achieving a regard for the truth which is, at least some of the time, greater than the desire not to suffer

These are all complex aspects of mental functioning and are not easy to measure even for the subject. Although there may sometimes be a specific presenting problem that can be resolved, the therapy will often trace back the roots of a specific problem into areas that could not have been foreseen at the outset. Mr X from Chapter 4 showed complex problems.

Mr X came to see a therapist because his ex wife wanted to deny him access to his little boy aged three. He was very attached to his child but was furiously angry with his ex wife whom he accused of all sorts of neglect and unworthiness. He said in the initial consultation that he hoped to be helped to become more able to help his little boy and, the therapist suspected, also to be more impressive to the courts about his suitability to have access. He was a large man who worked in a care home for older people and was full of the hardships that life had imposed on him. He began the early sessions by saying: 'It's happened again.' What had happened again was that someone or something had disappointed him or let him down in some way. He had taken his car for a service and was charged a large sum for various repairs. He then found that the fan belt needed replacing. He had to take the car back and this made him miss an important appointment. So no matter how hard he tries, he says that he can't get anything to work for him.

The therapist finds indications of pathology here which she thinks would need long therapy to affect if they could be affected at all. The most obvious difficulty is that everything seems to be referred to him. He is not psychotic but he refers behaviour of people and things to a deliberate slighting of his needs. For him a mechanic's error is not just an annoying mistake, it is an attack on him and another example of the way in which a malevolent universe seeks to undermine his efforts and make him suffer. Technically this is a narcissistic problem and most therapists, while expecting a degree of narcissism in all their patients, would worry about the likely outcome of working with such a level of self reference combined with obsessional thinking about the way in which others obstruct him.

One problem that immediately arises is that the patient and the therapist would have different views about what might constitute a cure in his case. He would not think of himself as cured unless his wife and everyone else stopped obstructing him and let the world be as he thinks it should be. On the other hand, the therapist would not think he was cured unless he was able to begin to see things sometimes from the point of view of another, or at least to be able to recognise that there is another point of view.

Curing Narcissus

Freud thought that treatment of narcissistic disorder was unlikely to be successful because there is no apparent transference. The person who, like the youth in the myth, is obsessed with gazing at his own image does not look up to see another person and therefore does not demonstrate patterns (see Chapter 3). If Narcissus will not look up from his own image, he cannot transfer any of his past onto anyone or anything other than his own image. If the curative effect of analytic work were based solely on the use of transference, this would clearly present a major problem unless we are able to do something with the very absence of the transference.

Freud pointed out that this lack of interest in the external world is something we all experience when we are physically ill and in pain. When the poet suffers from toothache:

> Concentrated is his soul
> In his molar's narrow hole
> (Busch quoted in Freud 1914: 75)

Fortunately, we all have to pass through a stage of primary narcissism and most of us emerge able to love another and cease to be totally self-obsessed. Freud calls this an object *choice* and this is an important hypothesis for analytic therapy. The narcissistic object choice which focuses entirely on the image of the self must still be seen to be a choice in some sense. The cure for the suffering that it causes will then be achieved when the patient reaches a point of being aware that he has a choice. Betty Joseph's patient mentioned in Chapter 3 was in a transference state that was difficult to pin down in relation to any one past experience, but when she heard his dream with its 'state of war' she was able to see that the beginning of a transference could be discerned here. Even though the narcissistic person is very difficult to reach and will not be likely to work well with an inexperienced therapist, there is now literature on how to work with such people. The techniques that are currently used can be classified in several groups:

- empathy and mirroring
- twinship and matters of identity
- interpretation of unconscious meaning below conscious material.

The first of these groups described by Heinz Kohut (1971) emphasises the importance of entering into the painful situation of the patient rather than trying to appear more clever and therefore appearing more grandiose If the therapist does seem to be trying to be clever, he will activate the grandiosity in the patient to an extent which engenders rage and is likely to bring the therapy to a disastrous end. The mirroring transference encompasses the patient's need to be recognised and affirmed by a parent and, in the therapeutic context, will demand recognition and affirmation. The therapist will have to judge very carefully how much of this to give and how to scale it down just as the good enough parent will so that there is neither feast nor famine. Twinship transferences are those in which the therapist faces a strong demand that she should be like the patient. This need for identification must be recognised and again given some space and gratification. One encouraging aspect of this transference is that seeking to make the therapist be as like you as possible is an attempt which shows some dawning recognition that there might be two people in the room and the therapist will need to work to nurture this without too much threat to the patient.

What is a Transference Cure?

For many people, the moment at which they commit themselves to a therapist is a turning point in their lives. They have suffered neurotic misery and not been able to find a way out or round their suffering on their own or through any family and friends they might have. In fact, family and friends are often unintentionally exacerbating the suffering by well meaning efforts to get the patient to cheer up or snap out of it. The relief that someone is finally willing to listen and not immediately require an improvement is in itself able to lift patients out of the worst of their depression at least temporarily. After all, everyone needs hope and hope may be just what the therapist can offer right at the beginning.

When a patient is full of hope and decides to place his faith in the ability of the therapist to help him, he is likely to idealise the person he has chosen. An idealising transference seems to be reminiscent of the faith that a child needs to be able to place in his parents, both mother and father who must be able to protect him and deal with the difficulties of life that he cannot yet manage for himself. We would not be surprised if the patient in therapy immediately reverts to something like this state of mind, wanting to be looked after and to be helped as he might have wished to be helped by his parents. Whether or not his parents were able to do this is not the point at issue. Adults have seen and known that some children receive this sort of care and they will wish for it even if they have had very little taste of it themselves.

In this state of potential and useful dependency, a patient is perhaps ready to listen but is also very vulnerable. The therapist does not set out to teach and is therefore not relying on the authority of her statements to make a difference. Nevertheless, her statements will have authority and in fact the more she is able to listen and keep quiet, the more her pronouncements when she does make them will count and will be considered and puzzled over by the patient who is compelled to find every drop of meaning in the rare draught being offered.

In this state, the patient is open to suggestion. The hypnotists who were having some success in the late nineteenth century, for example, in Paris under Charcot, had to acknowledge that their successes were often temporary. Their method consisted of making suggestions or in fact giving orders to patients under hypnosis. These orders were obeyed but the improvement that this brought gave no further insight into the problem that caused the symptom in the first place beyond the important indication that that it was under psychological control. Freud was paying particular attention to the degree of cure that could be achieved by psychoanalysis. He had seen that hypnosis as practised by Josef Breuer could bring about a relief of symptoms but he had also observed that the relief of symptoms was temporary. In 1905 he was convinced that the relief of symptoms was not enough:

> I gave up the suggestive technique and with it hypnosis so early in my practice because I despaired of making suggestions powerful and enduring enough to effect permanent cures. (1905: 261)

This does not mean that all of the symptom relief effected by hypnosis would disappear. The problem was that no-one knew why some cases were successful and others were not. Freud's own answer to this question was that successful treatment would be only that in which the repression of the precipitating thoughts was lifted and the roots of the fear that led to the repression were traced and made known to the ego. In other words, it would have to become conscious.

When Breuer told Freud of his work with hysterics, the road ahead seemed much clearer and it led away from hypnosis and suggestion. If the patient could be helped by tracing her symptoms back to the past and to her own wishes, then the analyst was not making suggestions of his own, he was merely responding to the patient's own material.

This is a problem for all forms of therapy, however and we cannot be confident that we have removed the possibility of suggestion merely by following the patient's material and not giving instructions. Silence in itself is a language that the therapist teaches the patient to interpret. He may become adept at hearing slight movements and there is a great difference between the silence of boredom and the silence of alert attention, between the silence of anger and the silence of approbation. Psychological research into reinforcement explains the phenomenon that the patient learns to bring the kind of material that brings some sort of response from his therapist. Jungian therapists find that their patients bring them Jungian dreams and Freudian patients soon begin to bring dreams with wishes that can be unearthed. In the same way, transference interpretation can itself suggest that symptoms are caused by the infantile experience and the patient who is in a receptive state can be eager to take up ideas which lead to a rapid but not well founded improvement. This sort of improvement is based in the transference to the longed for parent and constitutes what Freud calls the *transference cure*.

The primary motive force in any therapy is the patient's suffering and his wish to escape from it. He will respond to the attention of the therapist as if it were love:

> Often enough the transference is able to remove the symptoms of the disease by itself but only for a while, only for as long as it lasts. In this case the treatment is a treatment by suggestion and not psychoanalysis at all. It only deserves the latter name if the intensity of the transference has been used

for the overcoming of resistances. Only then has becoming ill
become impossible.   (1913: 143)

There were many problems with Freud's conclusions, not least
the difficulty of carrying out the therapy that was required. It
would inevitably take time. Freud saw his patients six days a
week, although he did allow that in 'slight cases' three times
might sometimes be sufficient.

Psychoanalysis is always a matter of long periods of time of
half a year or whole years or longer periods than the patient
expects.   (1913: 129)

Transference Makes the Patient Worse

Because the process of recognising transference involves giving
the patient scope to reproduce through re-enactment the people
and situations that have been most painful, both the therapist
and the patient must be prepared for the therapy to bring up
the worst that can be experienced. That is one reason why the
assessment process should include some enquiry into what that
worst might be and what therefore might be anticipated for the
transference to bring with it. Since transference is a form of repetition and, if we think that is true, we might ask the question:
how can repeating the most painful experiences that a person
has had help him to deal with the future?

This is not just a question about the process of therapy but
is a fundamental question about the way in which the human
mind seeks to cure itself of grief, shock and trauma. Repetition
is obviously painful but exhibits the wound that the therapist is seeking to help to cure. Only by seeing what is wrong,
examining the wound, and perhaps cleaning it or dressing it
can the doctor help with a physical problem. The physical
image is not entirely appropriate but does indicate that the
pattern must appear before the therapist and patient together
can hope to change it. The purposive aspect of repetition is
that there can be a different outcome from the occasions in
the past.

Transference as Anti-cure

Transference is a process of repetition and as such will have a conservative tendency to keep the patient in the state in which he comes. One of the most fascinating and difficult questions which must be addressed by all theoretical models is why does the patient repeat old patterns?

We know that patients who suffer from a relationship with an unfaithful woman will go and find just such a woman again. If we look at his past we will often find that he is recreating a sense of abandonment that he might have experienced with his mother or father in which, to a greater or lesser extent, he felt that he no longer counted with them. This may explain some of the mechanism of the repetition but it does not explain why it happens.

One possible explanation might lie in the human capacity to hope combined with the human capacity to put a mistaken degree of trust in our own powers. Chapter 2 introduced the ideas of Jacques Lacan. His emphasis on the capacity of the human child to perceive himself as powerful when he is still small and helpless arises in the mirror stage which is described in more detail on p. 42. In the, mirror stage lies his explanation for the illusional element of narcissism. Whether we trace it back to such images of infancy or not, the human mind has to deal both with our wish for power and control of our environment and our gradual acceptance of our vulnerability and lack of control which, of course, ends in the acceptance of the inevitability of one's own death.

In terms of repetition, we can still hold on to enough omnipotence to believe that we can change people and situations so we call them up again. Usually this process is unconscious. If you ask the patient why he or she does this self harming thing again, he will not be able to tell you. Marilyn Monroe in the film *Some Like it Hot* cannot explain why she falls in love with men who are no good. She just taps the side of her head and says 'not very bright I guess'. Many patients would at least initially share this inability to understand their own behaviour. We seem to feel safe with repetition – like children who want the same story every night. The adult who strays from the exact words of the previous telling will discover that the three year old or even the two year old will be vastly disappointed if there is a departure from the way the story was told last time. There seems to be some sense of control for the child who knows what is coming next. At the very least the child knows that there will be a resolution and the ending will be safe and everyone will live happily ever after with the wolf or the dragon or the giant safely killed. Perhaps the adult who repeats his painful and distressing experience again in a new context is hoping that this time the story will come out right. This time the bad guys will be defeated and the good will triumph.

There is another aspect of the compulsion to repeat. In seeking to understand transference and resistance we soon perceive that the transference is itself only a piece of repetition, and that the repetition is a transference of the forgotten past not only on to the therapist but also on to all the other aspects of the current situation. The need to repeat in the outside world is echoed by a need to repeat painful and difficult or loving and blissful experiences. The difficulty of this process is well known and any therapist will have experienced some aspects of it. The problems lie in understanding the nature of the experience that is being repeated and the reason why it might need to be repeated. Most of all it is problematic because of the patient's attachment to the repetition, which now replaces the impulse to remember. In fact not only does it replace any desire to remember, it constitutes an active resistance against remembering. We can hold onto beliefs with determination in the face of evidence. Even a negative pattern being repeated by projection of bad qualities onto the therapist leading to hatred and resentment of her power will be held with amazing tenacity. The patient may not be convinced otherwise even in the face of continuing evidence of the therapist's goodwill and willingness to be faithful to the process.

When this situation arises, the cure will have to be a cure of the transference situation.

How Can the Therapist Help?

Viviane Green (2003) writes of Inji Ralph's experience of working with an eight year old girl, Flora, who had been repeatedly sexually abused by her paedophile father, who was in prison at the time of the therapy. Her mother was denied access to her because it was unclear whether she had been involved in the abuse. She was placed with a foster mother and her birth mother was allowed supervised access once per term. She gave the therapist a very difficult experience in that she ran from the room and ran wildly around the clinic prompting other staff to ask the therapist what she was doing with her to make her run away like that. The counter-transference feelings of the therapist were not surprisingly anxiety and the feeling of being overwhelmed. Flora presented highly seductive and sexualised behaviour. Her play involved physical display of her body:

> She decided to pretend she was a dog – resulting in my constantly being faced with her bottom. When I said 'You really think I want to see your bottom,' she stopped and said quietly, 'No. I don't think that'. She returned to her ball game but seemed calmer.   (2003: 167)

Flora's self control improved and she was able, before the therapy finished, to express care and love for her therapist. Ralph imputes the improvement to the therapeutic effect of acting out the past situation in the therapy. This serves several purposes: the experience which is too dreadful or too difficult to be put into words, especially by a child, can be shown in action to the clinician. Feelings that are intolerable can be projected into the therapist. The therapist can then model thinking about what is happening, bearing it and being able to put words to it. Even more important though is the sense in which the experience can be developmental.

> Over time through the transference relationship with a constant new developmental object, Flora had an experience of being a wanted child, giving her a sense of a self that is valuable and lovable.   (2003: 175)

Time is one essential ingredient of the therapeutic process. It takes a whole lifetime to get into some of the difficulties that patients bring to therapy. It is not going to take five minutes to make a difference and change the patterns that have been followed for so long (see also Chapter 5). One interpretation can often be the fulcrum from which changes will follow but they will need to be repeated and reinforced in the way that the negative patterns were. The process of *working through* is essential if therapy is to have the lasting effects that can distinguish it from hypnosis.

When is the Transference Resolved?

Transference that holds the patient, still only partly conscious, in a state that he has experienced before puts him, as it does any one of us, in a vulnerable condition. A surgeon would not wish to leave a patient with an open wound halfway through an operation. How can we know when the wound is sufficiently well closed to resist future infections and the pressure to open itself again? In *How Much is Enough?* (Murdin: 2000) I wrote about the difficulty of judging this when the judgment is left to the therapist. Most often the patient will decide for himself and this ability to decide may be a sign of increasing health or it may be a sign that the resistance has not lifted and the patient is not willing to promote his own change and development. The therapist can make clear that she does not agree that it is time to end or she can agree instantly in the interests of promoting autonomy: 'it's good to choose'.

It may be good to choose but there is an obligation on the therapist to choose too and the therapist must choose from a position of informed professional judgment whether or not the patient is ready to leave. If she considers that the leaving is from a transferential resistance, she has a duty of care to the patient to make whatever interpretation she can of the behaviour:

> Mr X came to his session one day saying that he was thinking that for the sake of his son he should stop coming to therapy. The cost was not just in terms of money which he could ill afford, but also in terms of time since he had to come after work and this took time away from their 'quality time' together. He added 'I don't suppose you will miss me droning

on either'. The therapist was in a difficult position. On the one hand she would have been immensely relieved if he had chosen not to continue. She was doubtful at the beginning that she could help him and was still not sure that the therapy was making much difference. His wishing to leave was in fact confirmation that he was not making a therapeutic alliance. On the other hand, she knew that in his childhood he had been left alone in his cot and he remembered standing holding the bars, yelling for his mother who would not come. Perhaps he wanted to know whether his therapist had any wish to come and pick him up? At a very obvious level, the possibility to leave was acting within a transference, especially as he mentioned the need for 'quality time' which he needed in order to give it to his son.

On reflection, the therapist decided to say that she thought that he was anxious about being kept in the cot at the age of three and not making progress. He was worried that he was expected to climb out on his own and that his therapist would be glad if he did so because she would not have to answer his calls any more. He found this intervention very upsetting and broke down in tears. He decided to stay in therapy for a time, saying 'If someone is willing to listen, I need to say more'.

This was work in progress and since the patient had already done enough to trust the therapist, he was able to take the opportunity to work on longer. Sometimes, the well intentioned therapist can misunderstand the transference with disastrous results:

Ms A came to a male therapist complaining of fits of unexplained anger. She had been told by her line manager that she must find a way of controlling her moods because in her work with old people she was becoming unpredictable. She was very negative about therapy, complaining right from the beginning that the therapist was incompetent that just talking wasn't going to help her at all. Her childhood had been affected by a violent father who hit her mother and walked out when she was three and a half leaving her mother who was unable to manage her small daughter on her own and left her with her grandmother for much of her early childhood until she went to school.

After six sessions Ms A announced that she would not be coming any more. The therapist, who felt very inadequate with this patient, immediately responded that the patient was wishing to escape from the difficult feelings that were brought up in therapy. She thought that the patient should stay longer so that they could together 'deal with her anger'. The patient said that she did not see any prospect of dealing with her anger and the therapist was merely succeeding in making her angrier. The therapist of course was subduing her own anger rather than 'dealing with it' and the patient was sensing that she really wanted to get rid of her and leave her with a grandmother.

The patient stormed out and lodged a complaint against the therapist saying that she was incompetent and that she had tried to hold on to Ms A because she needed the money and could not do without the fee. The therapist was not found to have behaved unethically but was advised to return to supervision and work to find how best to 'deal with her counter transference'. Such angry patients are likely to engender feelings of anger and resentment in the therapist who considers it her professional duty to react by suppressing the feelings and trying extra hard to exhibit unconditional positive regard or at least neutrality. The patient who is ultra sensitive to rejection feels this response as hypocrisy and reacts even more angrily against it.

How could the therapist working with Ms A have dealt with this transference situation? The answer is difficult to find but must involve working within the existing transference situation which obviously must be understood by the therapist. Ms A had clear *borderline tendencies*. This is a term that is used for a state in which a person can function well enough to hold a job and continue in some relationships but the passion with which emotional states are experienced leads to powerful outbursts of anger and will be seen as so out of proportion as to be almost psychotic to other people. This state usually involves a string of failed or damaged relationships in which other people have not been able to cope with the rage that erupts. The sufferer will often escape from an unbearable reality through the use of drugs and alcohol. Excessive use of alcohol is a factor to consider as a possible signal of this state. The borderline state also implies a lack of the ability to discern shared reality in relationships. To other people and to the subject himself, the behaviour will seem irrational or even deluded.

Borderline Personality Disorder Features:

A tendency to lose touch with shared reality for brief periods
Failed relationships
Outbursts of anger that seem unreasonable to others
Self harming behaviours
Addictive behaviour.

The term *borderline* indicates that the patient is on the borderline between neurosis and psychosis. Juliet Mitchell points out that the hysteric of yesterday has become the borderline of today (2000: 124). In saying this she is emphasising the lack of clarity in the definition and diagnosis of the term 'borderline' It is often confused with narcissism as well in spite of Kenberg's painstaking distinctions (1985). His 'descriptive analysis' of the characteristics of each these conditions shows how much they overlap. Nevertheless, the overriding quality of the borderline state is anxiety and the patient usually manages to convey a high level of anxiety to the therapist (1985: 9). Some therapists might query the usefulness of attaching diagnostic labels of this sort. It is useful if it helps to determine the approach that might be most helpful to them. Mitchell gives the interesting example of the poet Anne Sexton who was rescued from a schizophrenic ward where she had been placed because her hysteria 'mimed' schizophrenia and was on the borderline of psychosis: 'with all the appropriate symptoms and behaviour which had become definitions of schizophrenia' (2000: 126).

Ralph Greenson (1978) writes about the borderline characteristic of losing 'object representations'. By this he means that
the patient cannot hold on to any good attachment to the figure
of the therapist in his mind. The same problem haunts his other
relationships outside and may contribute to a string of failed
relationships. For this reason one of the aims of analytic therapy
will be to enable the patient to achieve some sort of object con-
stancy or the ability to hold a sense of a good and continuing
object when the object is not physically present. Since destructive anger is often characteristic when the object is present, many
analysts have emphasised that what is needed is an emphasis on
the *real* as opposed to the *transference* relationship. Greenson
meant by that a flexibility that implies that the therapist uses
extra-analytic techniques such as 'management, support, education, control. . . .' (1978: 371). The most important aspect of
working with borderline patients is the need for honesty. The
patient is often super sensitive to hypocrisy and deceit, perhaps
because of past experience and can detect any falsity in the therapist. In this sense, the therapist has to be 'real'. This does not
necessarily imply departing from an analytic stance as Rosenfeld
(1965) and others have asserted.

Marsha Linehan wrote a handbook based on a cognitive
behavioural approach saying that the borderline syndrome does
have meaning. She hypothesises that sufferers are born with an
innate biological tendency to react more intensely to lower levels
of stress than others and that they have grown up in an environment which has not helped them to develop an ability to
tolerate stress and believe that they can recover from insults.
They have not been able to develop sufficient belief in themselves
and their ability to survive to be able to manage the difficulties
of relationship. This is in line with the analytic definition which
emphasises poor self image and a weakness of the ability to
integrate and feel that there is a whole self.

The confusing message which someone suffering from this
mental state is encapsulated in the phrase:

> I hate you. Don't let me go.

The therapist trying to manage an ending with someone who
will ragefully defend this position is obviously fraught with

difficulty. Another attribute makes the resolving of transference even more difficult: the borderline tendency implies a need for constant crises and drama. This hunger for activity which might hide a hunger for change is likely to lead to threats to leave. The therapist will be tempted to give in to the threats or to resist interpreting the reason for them. Interpretations are likely to be met with anger and disbelief. The options for the therapist cluster around the possibility of paying attention to the profoundly uncomfortable counter-transference, and out of that, saying something about the suffering of Ms A who cannot feel that being with the therapist makes her feel better but also dreads not being with her. She could perhaps also say that the desire to leave is partly Ms A's need to test the ability of the therapist to find something good in her which would make a reason for staying.

Such an approach leads to the obvious question: what does it mean to resolve the transference?

Resolving the Transference

This is the process that is much sought by analytic therapists but rarely achieved in a recognisable state. There are two main outcomes, both of which are desirable for the patient. The first possibility is that the patient and therapist both recognise the nature of the pattern that is being transferred. In the case of Ms A this might mean that she was able to see that her experience with her own mother was likely to form a filter for the experience that she was having with her 'useless therapist'. For some people this might be enough to enable them to step outside the transference and begin to see that the therapist might indeed at times be incompetent but she did not deserve the whole of the transferred anger from the mother who had failed the child. Even more useful might be a recognition that the mother too might not have been wholly bad.

Alternatively, if that level of insight and self awareness cannot be achieved, the patient might be able to find a resolution within the transference. Ms A might be able to retain her almost delusional conviction that the therapist was just like her mother and within that come to a conviction that the therapist had some

good points even if only her reliability and willingness to perse-
vere. James Strachey, in his paper on mutative interpretations
written in 1952, considered that the analyst must continuously point out the difference between his actual behaviour
and the primitive superego full of harsh and cruel judgment
which the patient will project on to him. This is not easy to do
until the patient can hear what is being said and opens enough
to let it make a difference.

The main thrust of some of the person centred therapies is
to provide what looks like a corrective emotional experience.
Deficits in the loving care of the parents for the infant have left
the adult with emotional needs. Those who see supplying those
needs as the purpose of therapy will try to give a warm accepting response to the patient in an attempt to make up for what
was missing in the past. This approach is also seen as justify-
ing the use of touch, usually in the form of physically holding
the patient or hugging at times when he feels particularly in
need of comfort. There must, of course, be many safeguards in
place to ensure that this approach is not allowed to become abusive or exploitative. While this deficit model of therapy has a
place, it may leave the patient perhaps dependent on more of
the same and does not provide him with the tools to help himself in the future. While warmth and care have their place in
analytic work too, they will provide only what Donald Winnicott called 'nursing care' for the patient who is too disturbed to
endure the deprivation of analytic work. It clearly may have its
place for anyone suffering from extreme emotional distress. The
analytic therapies are seeking to resolve and dissolve what has
been harmful in its persistence from the past through illumina-
tion of the dark side of the mind. The positive experiences which
we offer will be in the reliability, the honesty and the care of
the therapist who will survive a tirade or cold blast of anger one
day and still say 'See you next time'. This is certainly a sort of
corrective emotional experience and, together with a careful but
open attempt to find the structures of the mind that are causing unnecessary problems, may enable the patient to come the
closest that he will get to cure. We know that analytic therapy
will not cure all ills but it must always offer *care* and care itself
heals.

Conclusion

Any therapist who works for a number of years is likely to come across a transference which is powerful and demanding and calls for levels of tolerance and understanding well beyond the usual. These people are likely to be in the group to which we give the short hand designation of *borderline patients*. In this chapter we have considered how these patients present and how they may be demonstrating patterns from the past. Providing what they need is a matter of both skill and experience and also to some extent a matter of temperament. Everyone can learn the theoretical background and the appropriate management techniques; not everyone has the warmth combined with open honesty that makes therapy bearable for these distressed people.

Discussion Points

1. A patient Mrs Smith (aged 35) comes to see a therapist describing moderate depression. She is taking time off work because she was not promoted and she feels that she has been overlooked by her manager. She does not get up until midday and feels that nothing is worth bothering about. Her mother suffered from clinical depression and committed suicide when Mrs Smith was eight. She was brought up by her grandmother. She has no siblings and seems isolated. She says that she has never had a sexual relationship and thinks that men are not interested in her. She says; I don't blame them. I am not very interested in myself'. She cries often during the assessment session. Mrs S asks you 'can you make me better?' What will you say?

2. In what sense are you offering a corrective emotional experience?

3. Do patients have the right to expect to be cured?

7 Ethical Problems

Questions to Consider While Reading

1. Why should the reliability of memory concern the analytic therapist?
2. How should a therapist deal with recovered memories of sexual abuse?
3. What are the components of an ethical therapeutic relationship?

Responsibility should accompany power. The analytic therapist has the responsibility to use wisely the power that is granted to her by virtue of the analytic method and its power to do good. Of course, if it can do good, it can also do harm. It is a very powerful tool, and the position held by the one who sits in the chair, is usually regarded by patients as being authoritative. At any rate, the patient wishes it to be so, and, as we know, will try to make his wish into reality. This chapter is about the problems that power can bring to the therapist who must always put the welfare of the patient first and genuinely wishes to do so, but does not always know how.

Analytic therapy rests on the assumption that there is truth and value in the hypothesis that we are formed by our experience as well as by genetic inheritance and that we can be helped to escape from the restrictions imposed by past experience by coming to understand the nature of what affected us so much that we still interpret the present in its light. The previous chapter considered the extent to which the analytical therapist is able to provide the degree of improvement that the patient comes to find. This chapter will look at the ethical problems that can arise in the process itself.

Remembering the Past or Making it Up

The process of discovery may be demanding and may be open to errors. Patients arrive at a better understanding of themselves through a process of recall combined with a process of creating a narrative that makes sense of memory and of the present. Freud described what he had at first hoped was the process of 'reconstruction' but later came to recognise as in fact often *construction* (1937). The aim of analytic work is to enable the patient to react to experiences and the emotions called up by them in a way which is more suited to the adult that he has become instead of in the way that the infant reacted. This means that the task of the analytical practitioner is 'to make out what has been forgotten from the traces which it has left behind or more correctly, to construct it' (quoted in Ellman 1991: 243). In addition to putting the construction of the past to the patient, the therapist will, according to Freud's instructions also explain how she arrived at it and will also consider very carefully what her timing should be:

> It is perfectly true that psychoanalysis, like other psychotherapeutic methods, employs the instrument of suggestion (or transference). But the difference is this: that in analysis it is not allowed to play the decisive part in determining the therapeutic results. It is used instead to induce the patient to perform a piece of psychical work – the overcoming of his transference resistances – which involves a permanent alteration in his mental economy. The transference is made conscious to the patient by the analyst, and it is resolved by convincing him that in his transference-attitude he is re-experiencing emotional relations which had their origin in his earliest object-attachments during the repressed period of his childhood. In this way the transference is changed from the strongest weapon of the resistance into the best instrument of the analytic treatment. Nevertheless its handling remains the most difficult as well as the most important part of the technique of analysis.   (Freud 1921)

The therapist can be compared with the archaeologist. From a variety of small fragments of pot or bone, she can put together the meaning or story that the fragments tell. She does not just make it up, she has good reasons to see how the pieces fit together and she must use the most reliable available methods to verify her assumptions. The therapist has the most helpful tool at her command and that is the transference which will demonstrate how the pieces will fit together into a meaning in the present. The archaeologist has finished his work when he has completed the reconstruction but the analyst is just at the beginning since each piece of material that is put in place must be followed by more pieces and further reinterpretation. Linking the present to the past is useful only in so far as the patient is able to elaborate the meaning that emerges and extend it into other new areas. We never can judge an interpretation by the patient's assent or dissent alone, but through the subsequent material that is brought which alone can show whether the interpretation was useful. As long as she is willing to listen to what the patient says following the constructions or interpretations, the dangers of suggestion will be minimised. Most practitioners would recognise that the story that gets told cannot be exactly a matter of historical truth but must have germs of truth in order to be useful.

Research has shown that there is another reason why finding the meaning that emerges should be considered to be a process of construction rather than reconstruction. Human memory is dynamic and is not a locked filing cabinet that stays the same over time. Recent studies of memory have shown clearly that subjects in experiments are influenced by subsequent events in the process of recall. For example Elisabeth Loftus et al (1978) have recounted experiments in which subjects were given incorrect information after an event and then firmly 'recalled' that false information. In one experiment subjects were shown a scene with a STOP sign in it. They were then told that it was a YIELD sign. Eighty per cent of the subjects later recalled the scene with the YIELD sign. The discussion of this experiment emphasises the way in which the material was presented to the subjects and may be an effect of the order in which the scenes were presented. It may also be affected by the way in which the false information is given. If the person who gives the false information is trusted and authoritative, the subject is likely to create a new record in memory which will be the one to be found when the memory is searched. The implication for the therapist is that she is in a position to suggest a different scene in the past from the one that was originally produced and the new version might be substituted and become the only record available.

Recovered Memories

Analytic therapy encourages patients to retrieve memories that they might have repressed. Psychoanalysis was based on the belief that the hysterical patient Anna O as Freud and Breuer called her (1883) was suffering from repressed memories. Breuer who was treating her took fright when she produced a fantasy that she was pregnant and that Breuer, her analyst, was the father. This is a demonstration of the passionate involvement that may be required of a therapist by a patient who, in her case, was trying to evade her own guilt for her wishes towards her father this degree of involvement is naturally disturbing, even frightening to a therapist whose career may seem to be threatened. Nevertheless, the area of sexual fantasy and sexual abuse has a long history of causing pain and distress to the one who was abused and considerable difficulty to therapists.

Because some patients may consult therapists when they feel that an experience of sexual abuse in the past is affecting life in the present, therapists may be called upon to work out what their own role in the unfolding story must be. The British False Memory Society alleges that therapists have not only encouraged patients to confront family members with accusations but also have actually implanted 'memories' of abuse which did not happen. Given the unreliability of memory as described by, for example, Sandler and Fonagy (2000) and the way in which memories can be constructed, the position of the therapist is perhaps best seen as empathic neutrality. While retaining her ability to show that she can feel for the patient's continuing suffering, the therapist needs to refrain from committing herself to complete acceptance of the historical verisimilitude of the memories. The therapist cannot know what happened in the past. That does not mean that she does not believe her patient. On the contrary, she believes the emotional truth of what she hears but she has to reserve her judgment about the historical, factual truth which she can never be sure that she knows. In the transference derived from the parent who might not have believed the patient, there will often be great pressure to affirm unquestioning belief in what she is being told. All she can do is reiterate her belief in the importance of the patient's experience and its effect on the present. She cannot in honesty and with an ethical stance say that she believes that x or y happened in objective reality.

At the heart of the analytic process therefore the analyst is encouraging the patient to settle on a story which makes sense of the present through giving new meaning to a version of the past. The whole reason for the presence of the analyst in this process is that she will be able to see and put forward a different view of the patient's meaning from the one which the patient has been able to find for herself. She must stop short of changing the STOP sign to YIELD. The therapist has to deal with the paradox of her situation. In order to help the patient at all, she must be allowed to take up the position of the 'one who knows' in the mind of the patient to the extent that she will be trusted. This may be described as the position of the parent or the lover but is usually a position in which wisdom is ascribed to the analyst and her words are given authority and whether overtly accepted or rejected, are nevertheless, of great influence.

There are therefore two main areas of ethical responsibility for the practitioner, especially for those who work with transference.

- First is the formation of the trusting alliance with some part of the patient. This must be an ethical relationship.
- Second is the use of the powerful and influential tool of constructing the biography of each individual in a way that gets as close to the truth as possible. This must be the ethical use of technique.

Forming a Relationship that is Ethical

'The patient knows what he is getting into'
'Caveat emptor' 'Let the buyer beware'

These attitudes to the position of the patient approaching a therapist imply that the patient knows or can find out what he is getting into. In fact, there is good reason to think that he does not and usually cannot know this. This difficulty with free choice has been thoroughly examined by Robert Hinshelwood (1967) in *Therapy or Coercion*. He points out that the patient by definition is not able to judge his own needs and his own wishes. He has come because of a sickness of the mind often interfering with his power of judgement. The functions that the ego performs are not being carried out normally. He may not be able to relate well to the external world. He cannot see reality as his friends, relatives or colleagues perceive it. How then could we expect that he will be able to judge his own therapeutic needs?

The second point that Hinshelwood makes very cogently is that the patient is not able to form an alliance with the doctor over the kind of treatment needed. The doctrine that there is a healthy part of the patient that can form an alliance with him is very widely held but requires belief in a degree of health which is often not perceptible. Certainly the patient needs a degree of understanding that therapy might help him or alternatively, a perverse belief that he can destroy the therapy and with it any need to make an effort on his own behalf. Hinshelwood's view of the therapeutic process is analogous to that of the surgeon operating for appendicitis. He is wounding in order to heal. He has the patient's overall consent to carry out the procedure but has to make the patient unconscious before he can use the knife to open up the abdominal cavity and begin the procedure. The patient arriving for a first session of therapy may be in some ways as unconscious as the patient undergoing a surgical procedure. The truth is that the therapist must make him gradually more conscious and aware of his pain because that will be the route that he must take to an improved awareness of his own capacity to change himself and his life.

The more the therapist can bring together the parts of the personality by integration, the more he is enabling the patient to make an informed judgment about whether he wishes to continue with therapy. At the beginning, the unconscious will play a major part in the process of choosing a therapist and this will be operative in the choices of both patient and therapist but we have to work to make sure that the therapist is more consciously aware of her motives than the patient can be.

Because of the importance of the transference in the first meeting, the therapist must make a judgment about when to make an interpretation or comment about the patient's possible unconscious links to the therapist and to the process of therapy in the first meeting. Since many people make initial appointments to see several therapists so that they can 'choose' which one to see, there may be only one opportunity to speak to a prospective patient who does not choose to return and continue. If someone comes with an unrealistic wish or a wish that does not relate to what the therapist sees as the problem, there may be a question about how much to say.

> Ms S came to see a therapist saying that she wanted to be more able to take time for herself because her family made too many demands on her. The therapist was concerned when she discovered that the family consisted of a baby of seven months and a young toddler of two. The father was present and seemed to contribute to the housework, doing all the cooking at weekends, but Ms S felt that she needed more time 'to be me'. Her husband worked full time while she did not work outside the home. The therapist thought that her fear of demand needed to be understood but did not agree that the aim of the therapy would be to help Ms S to remove the demand. Two young children need to be able to make demands on their mother. She did not say that she thought this, but did say that she thought that Ms S would be helped by a greater understanding of her feelings about the needs of her two young children. She agreed that this was important and seemed to be willing to look at this aspect of the problem.

The therapist may disagree with the patient's formulation of what is wrong with him, especially when the patient may sometimes use whatever is current in the media to describe what he thinks is his diagnosis. Experiments on suggestibility show that adults can be convinced of a suggested truth:

> Indeed it is hard to think of any other explanation for the hundreds of cases who according to John Mack, the Harvard psychiatrist can recover memories of having been abducted by alien visitors from space, or for the remarkable outbreak in America of something like 20,000 cases of Multiple

Personality Disorder (MPS) since 1980 or for the belief held by some therapists that hypnosis can reach memories from *earlier* lives. (Sandler and Fonagy 1997: 14)

The interest in MPS had a spurt of books and articles published in the popular press. For a while there was heightened interest in the United States particularly and many patients wondered whether the sense of alienation or 'not feeling myself' which so often accompanies mental suffering could be caused by a version of multiple personality disorder. The popularity of this syndrome has faded away in the twenty first century. Patients seek a dramatic and satisfying illness to describe their symptoms. On the other hand, it has little actual explanatory power and even less therapeutic implication.

We have to accept that there are fashions in diagnosis. Not only are patients susceptible to thinking that they have whatever they last read about in the Sunday papers, but also therapists are inclined to look for and find signs of whatever they have recently read or discussed. Therapists of course have knowledge and experience that they don't leave outside the consulting room and they should be able to see when they are dealing with a particular syndrome and when they are not. There will also be pressure from the patient to accept a particular view of what is wrong. Analytic therapists of all people should be suspicious of the conscious conclusions that their patients have reached. They should be asking what else is going on since our theory states that the ego is always likely to be subverted by the unconscious. They are nevertheless human and subject to the need to earn a living and to keep at least some of the patients who come to them.

Patients coming for an assessment might in the twenty first century find that they suffer from ME (Myolagic Encephalitis). Therapists, on the other hand, may think that this is shorthand for some form of hysterical refusal. The body may be helping the patient to express an unconscious reluctance to allow a certain action or set of actions to take place. The weakness of the body and the exhaustion of ME is a most painful and unpleasant syndrome and it may or may not have a discoverable psychological cause. Most therapists would want to explore whether the patient had come to a therapist because he or she had some inkling that the physical state was in some way connected with their mental and emotional state. The therapist will want to know the history and the emotional map of the patient who may well be angry if the therapist seems to want to interpret the illness away or imply that the patient could choose to be well by a conscious act of will.

Patients come with phrases from the media such as 'I need time and space for me' and 'I need to work out what *I* need so that I do not spend all my time looking after others. It's time to look after myself'. In this situation therapists may recognise a narcissistic state which is mixed with a genuine inability in the patient to know his own wishes and desires. In any case, the effect of the therapy is likely to be to help the patient to see what another is thinking or feeling and not to impose care on the other person or to remove it. The effect in other words may be exactly the opposite of what the patient is demanding. The blind demand will be changed into conscious desire and will be therefore subject to conscious choice. The therapy will work to achieve what is often summed up as the aim of psychoanalysis: Where id was, there ego shall be.

Is it ethical for the therapist to embark on therapy with a different idea of what the therapy may achieve from that of the patient? In transference terms, the patient wishes to continue with the pattern of making a demand and having it denied. The therapist wishes to change the course of the demand and make sure that the patient in future knows what he wants and will be able to achieve it through loving and being loved, not through hopeless demands. Nevertheless, there is a requirement that all therapy tends to support truth and the recognition of what is rather than what we wish to be the case. How much therefore should the therapist inform the patient about what she thinks will happen in the therapy?

Bearing this question in mind, the therapist offering to begin therapy has an ethical responsibility to ensure that she has as much consent from the patient as he or she is able to give. For this to happen, the patient must know as much as he can at the outset. Some therapists choose to convey facts in the form of an initial information sheet or verbal information about the nature of analytic therapy. Neither process is likely to give the patient much useful information about what to expect because the therapist does not know what any given person will have to deal with. All that can be said is that there is likely to be some emotional distress in the process. Whatever was painful in the past may have to be revisited. The patient agreeing to a surgical procedure knows that the recovery will involve some physical pain but cannot know what that will mean before it happens. Pain is relative. Some people can accept physical conditions that are painful to others as being a minor inconvenience. Analgesics have much more effect for some people than others and so the recovery process will be much more difficult for some than for others.

In the same way, of course, we cannot know what an individual will need to experience in therapy before it begins. All we can say with any certainty is that some painful experiences may need to be revisited and that during the therapeutic process the patient may feel as bad as he ever has. This emphasises the need to enquire during assessment about what is the worst state that the patient has ever experienced so that the therapist is forewarned of the dangers, whether they are suicidal tendencies, self harm, manic depressive states or other neurotic symptoms. The therapist needs to know whether there may be a need to contact a physician and may need to know whether she has permission to contact the physician or whether she must do so only in cases of emergency when she judges it necessary to do so without permission. The therapist's role *in loco parentis* will be discussed on page 155–156.

Forming a Therapeutic Alliance

If a therapist intends to try to be a blank screen on which the patient can project his transference images, then she will have to make a value judgment about what constitutes a blank screen. Does it imply neutrality and a refusal to side with any one part of the patient's personality against another? Does it also imply silence which might suggest a lack of humanity in the therapist to the beginning patient? Some therapists do undoubtedly think that they should minimise the extent to which they show a response to the patient of any sort. To most people this could come across as cold and ungiving. This in itself will have transference implications in that the patient may have known a parent who was silent or absent and the therapist will be located in the negative arena at once. This may be what the patient needs but in many cases, he will not be able to see that he needs it or that it could lead to a positive outcome if he is willing to stay. In many cases the patient will just not stay with the therapist who is perceived in this way, especially if he also goes to interview a more open or apparently helpful therapist. This poses a moral dilemma in that a therapist could be tempted to be more welcoming in the first session than she will be on subsequent occasions in order to entice a patient to continue. This could be justified on the grounds that if the patient needs help to begin with, the therapist should give help so that in the long term she can do the analytic work.

Ethical Developments

At the beginning of therapy, it may be wise to emphasise the positive aspect of working through painful experiences again. Telling the patient that the therapy may unearth some painful thoughts is one way of preparing for this. Some therapists would go as far as to pick out the encouraging and positive aspects of the patient's story saying things like: 'It must have taken a lot of courage to come here today'. If this sort of encouragement is given only at the first session it may then leave the patient starving for want of more and also perhaps a little confused about why his therapist chose to be so affirming at first but then would not give him a word of encouragement later. On the other hand, some models of therapy would advocate giving that kind of encouragement throughout. For transference based work, this would put the therapist too firmly into the role of desirable parent, leaving out the negative. It would also put the therapist in the role of one who knows, one who can judge the value of behaviours.

This consideration naturally raises the question: how does a practitioner know when the transference needs interpreting and when it should be left to develop and mature? Freud (1916) recommended that one of the first tasks of the analyst is to establish a treatment alliance with the patient. Doing so probably means that the positive transference will not be interpreted but will be left to enable the patient to work with the difficulties and deprivations which the analytic work inevitably brings. Signs of warmth and interest in the patient are noted and may be encouraged to an extent which enables the patient to attach to the analyst as he would to a loving and nurturing mother. Practitioners of other models sometimes accuse analytic practitioners of tantalising behaviour. Is encouraging the transference fully in accordance with ethics which place the well being of the patient at the top of all priorities? We can argue that it is morally desirable only if we are as sure as we can be that the therapy will do more good than harm.

The encouragement of positive transference will more often take the form of not interpreting the hidden negative ideas, rather than active encouragement of it. Active encouragement of negative transference could involve retaliation and overt expression of anger or impatience, any of which would be unprofessional apart from the very occasional circumstances in which a patient needs to be stopped from destructive behaviour. Occasionally a practitioner may wish to point out the positive that lies behind negative behaviour. This happened during the early sessions of Mr A when his therapist was about to go on holiday:

> Mr A, a young accountant, has been seeing a psychotherapist for two months when she decides that it is time to tell him about her next holiday in a month's time. He says, on being told of Mrs B's holiday 'Well I'm really glad you're having some time off. I shall be able to fit in some time at the gym more easily when I am not coming to these sessions at nine o'clock'. The practitioner recognises the reality but also hears the pain behind the nonchalance: 'I can see that it will be much more convenient for going to the gym and you can exercise your body there but perhaps you will miss the opportunity to work out your feelings and thoughts here with me. You always protected your mother from letting her know that you minded when she spent time with your younger brother and I don't suppose you would complain to me either'.

This sort of interpretation is likely to increase the positive feelings although it allows the patient scope to deny what at this early stage of the work is likely to feel to him like unsafe dependency on his practitioner. It can be said to be a necessary interpretation in that there are clearly hidden feelings which the practitioner could understand from the tone of voice, the determined cheerfulness with which the comment was made and most of all from the material about his childhood which the patient had told her. Would a non-analytic practitioner agree that this sort of interpretation is ethical? A person centred practitioner would probably disapprove of it. It goes beyond the patient's own conscious awareness and makes a suggestion to which of course, the patient may either assent or dissent. The authority of the practitioner makes it difficult for a new patient to dissent overtly but the dissent in the unconscious will certainly make itself known. This above all is the justification for such an interpretation. If it were not made, much hidden longing and resentment from the past would stay hidden to emerge unbidden and cause the patient problems in his current relationships. If he can allow it to bring thoughts or associations to his mind and if he can speak his mind, the effect may be to open new areas of association and to show him the roots of some of his behaviour. If he chooses to continue to protect his therapist and himself from the truth, other opportunities will have to be seized for working on this aspect of his behaviour.

If, on the other hand, at this early stage in therapy, the therapist had gone straight for the negative in Mr A's statement, she might have frightened him away. She might for example have said: 'I think you are angry with me for abandoning you but you do not wish me to know because somehow my ignorance of your true feelings gives you back a sense of the power which my break makes you feel that you lack.' Such a response might have been helpful if there was already a strong alliance working between them but could have made it difficult for him to stay because it effectively makes him even more powerless by referring to his tendency to feel small in relation to the therapist who is his powerful mother or father in transference terms.

The Ethical Use of Technique: When to Interpret Transference

Since Freud mainly saw transference in terms of resistance, he advocated interpreting transference only when it manifested itself as resistance to the fundamental rule of free association. Following this rule would mean that the therapist refrains from the beginner's tendency to think 'I've seen it, so I'll say it'. It means that the therapist ought to think very carefully about what she hopes to achieve by the statement of a transference link which she thinks she has seen.

This chapter has already made reference to the importance of timing. While timing is itself a matter of competence, it does also have ethical implications. No-one should practise analytic therapy which is a powerful and, therefore, potentially dangerous instrument unless they have the best training that they can find and have worried and puzzled over the usefulness of what they are doing. Even then, the question of competence should always be in the back of their mind. Each therapist will have to ask at times: 'Am I well enough to see people?' Eventually, we will all have to say: 'Am I too old to be useful to people any more?' Above all, each therapist has to ask at the beginning: 'Am I skilled enough to see this person?' The trouble is of course that at the beginning of therapy the therapist cannot know exactly what will be required of him or her and therefore will find it difficult to say whether she is skilled enough. The help of a more experienced colleague in the role of supervisor is always desirable when beginning work with a new patient. It takes considerable humility to be willing to say that a patient may need someone more skilled and it may have to be done in the face of opposition from the patient who has decided that once he has told his story he has no wish to move on to another therapist.

At the threshold of analytic therapy the transference can be regarded as a major diagnostic tool and the practitioner will face ethical questions in handling it responsibly. The rule might need to be one of restraint. If there is any doubt about the purpose of speaking, then wait. The practitioner is under constant pressure to satisfy narcissistic needs and may rush to make a transference interpretation for all sorts of conscious reasons, some of which may be traceable back to narcissistic needs of her own. She will at times feel helpless or incompetent and the pressure then comes both from the patient and from herself to be able to 'do' something. Not to feel this might indicate an element of sadism or indifference to suffering. But delivering an interpretation is a serious business and must always be done for reasons that relate to the benefit of the patient. Of course such a statement begs the question of how we know what will benefit the patient. The answer has to be that we often cannot be certain but theory leads us halfway and knowledge of the individual patient must lead to the rest. When the doubt is considerable, consultation with a senior colleague will be essential.

When the analyst considers that the patient is repeating childhood conflicts, then she will interpret the transference. The patient has only one instruction from the outset of therapy: to say what comes into his mind. If he is finding it difficult to say what he is thinking, he is clearly resisting this primary rule of analytic therapy and an interpretation of why he might be doing so will be at the heart of the therapeutic process for him. Often the patient can speak freely in the first session and tells his story. The second session is more difficult because the story has been told and, from now on, the logical, rational patient does not know what is expected of him or what will please his therapist. In most cases, he tries to come up with something interesting and waits to see the effect. Sometimes he can manage nothing more than an embarrassed silence. This is a situation in which the therapist may speak in order to try to understand what is holding him back and in order to help him to make use of the new experience of therapy.

One good reason for interpreting transference therefore is to enable the patient to make use of therapy. Reverting to the forms of defence of the small child may well involve silence because the small child may have the belief that if he is silent, he will be invisible too. The resistance itself can be seen as part of an infantile pattern resulting from the felt need for defence against the parent. Transference, like an onion offers itself in layers and must not be pulled away too quickly, or, like an unfolded onion, it may leave nothing at its heart. The analyst therefore must resist the temptation to go on picking off the layers too enthusiastically by identifying herself in each piece of material. When the transference itself appears to be hiding something and preventing the work from progressing, only then is it legitimate, necessary in fact, to remove its defensive power by interpreting it.

Self Revelation

The question of the extent to which a practitioner should reveal details of her own life is another area that is both a matter of technique and a matter of ethics. In order to enable the relationship to develop a positive pole, some therapists might be tempted to talk about themselves so that they can say things like 'I had the same experience, I know just how you feel'. This is a temptation to be resisted because such a comment would set up an illusion of identity which would not be helpful. Because therapy above all seeks emotional truth. Such an identification also suggests the possibility of a friendly conversation rather than the analytic relationship which has to remain professional and has to retain some distance. The question of whether to reveal one's self may arise only in unusual circumstances, as for example when the therapist is planning to go into hospital and will need to take time off. Sometimes the therapist suffers a bereavement and will not be able to function as well as normal. Should she tell the patient what is the matter when, for example, she takes a day to go to a funeral?

The clear answers to these questions relate to the need for the therapist to be a neutral presence for the patient who is felt to be strong enough to withstand attacks and negative feelings of all sorts. If the therapist is ill or appears to be in need of sympathy, that might lead to a reaction from the patient and might inhibit his ability to speak of his own problems or depend appropriately on the therapist. On the other hand, if the therapist is ill, the truth may need to be confronted. If the problem is expected to be transitory, the patient may well be required to deal with it. The therapist may be confident that she has a virus which will pass and then she will feel able to deal with the patient's anger but for a short time she was not up to giving him what he needed. On the other hand, if the illness is serious or even terminal, she may have to tell him even though she does not anticipate being well again for him. He will have to deal with her reality and the truth will be the anchor for both patient and therapist. Circumstances of serious illness will be extremely difficult and painful for both and will bring up for the patient other experiences of illness or death. He may be able to transfer to another therapist and work with someone stronger on what has happened.

Those are occasions when there is little choice but to be open with the patient. There are other occasions when the choice is more difficult. At the outset of therapy, many patients need to know what are the limits of confidentiality that they will receive. A statement like the following will be enough for many patients:

> I shall treat what you tell me as confidential. I do have consultations with a supervisor who is a senior practitioner and will certainly also respect total confidentiality.

Ethical problems arise if the patient then asks for the name and qualifications of the supervisor. Does the patient have the right to know this? Most people would think not and in fact there may be an argument that it would be a betrayal of the supervisor's right to privacy in the European Union under Human Rights legislation.

The therapist will have a dilemma in answering this question because she may not wish to begin the relationship by refusing to answer what seems like a reasonable question. The answer may have to be confined to saying that the consultant has a right to privacy unless he or she has specifically agreed to be identified.

Sexual Relationships

Transference is a powerful tool. Like any form of power, it can be used for good or ill. Specific ethical issues arise for the practitioner who considers that transference is a valuable instrument and seeks to use it therapeutically. If a patient is under the influence of a positive transference and is idealising the practitioner, she may have the opportunity to abuse the trust and the compliance that will arise. Such abuse can take the form of exploitation in financial terms or it may lead to a sexual relationship. All ethical codes for psychoanalysts and psychotherapists include the prohibition against sexual relationships during the therapeutic process. Christopher McKenna writes vividly of the devastation brought about by an analyst who had entered into a homosexual relationship with his patient and had therefore confused the literal with the symbolic in a 'nightmare world' in which there were no longer any secure boundaries between inner and outer (2003: 53). Christian Gaillard lists what he thinks are some of the essentials of an ethical therapeutic relationship:

> The second ethical requirement of an analysis is to mourn our essentially incestuous impulses to withdraw into the lively enchanting joys of an interior animation that would love to ignore both time and history. (2003: 84)

If she is to mourn the loss of the possibility of a sexual relationship with the patient, the therapist too will have to rework her own oedipal renunciation. She must recognise her wish to possess the patient as her oedipal love object as defined by Harold Searles (1965). The patient may fulfil all sorts of needs for the analyst but the generic need for all of us is to find the substitute for mother or father who will love unconditionally and unquestioningly. The patient will at times do just that. To refuse oneself the satisfaction that this offers is a hard task. Nevertheless, the therapist must be clear that she must at all times deny herself the satisfaction of whole or partial gratification.

Creating a warm and accepting environment for the patient is fraught with difficulties because the analyst has her own emotions, some of which may arise from transference. One of the most famous cases that we know is that of Sabina Spielrein and her love for Carl Jung. A recent study of Spielrein (Covington and Wharton 2003) as a psychoanalyst in her own right emphasises her contribution to the theory of psychoanalysis in that she wrote about the destructive element in love. Both Freud and Jung developed some ideas that they derived from her. Freud elaborated the idea of the inevitable destructiveness into the fullblown theory of the death instinct. Spielrein had much reason to know about the destructiveness of love since she fell in love with Carl Jung and he seems to have responded enough to give her some hope although Coleen Covington (2003: 1) begins by saying that it is doubtful whether their relationship was ever consummated, What does seem to be documented is that she was the first patient to be treated by the psychoanalytic method by Jung. She appears to have got better and was discharged from hospital in 1905 as 'better' but remained in treatment with Jung as an outpatient for another four years. Although Jung may not have gone so far as to have a physical relationship with his patient, he certainly let her know that he loved her and was sufficiently anxious to ask Freud's advice as did Spielrein herself. This prompted Cremerius to write in his foreword to Caratenuto's account (*Tagebuch einer heimlichen Symmetrie*):

> It is a terrible story, particularly as it demonstrates the complicity of two men against the woman who has allowed herself to be seduced by one of them.   (2003: 63)

In order for this 'terrible story' to happen, Jung had abandoned the realm of fantasy and symbol and had ignored his duty to see and interpret her feelings for him as arising from transference. Instead he had allowed his own transferred feelings to becomes first affectionate and then passionate and had not attempted to interpret his own feelings. As a result Jung was precipitated into a potential scandal to the extent that he wrote to the patient's mother to assure her that he was the doctor and not the lover of her daughter. In order to make this clear he raises the question of a fee, as he had not been charging a fee for his private consultations but from now on intends to do so: 'the doctor knows his limits and will never transgress them because he is paid for his trouble' (2003: 66).

Some of the cases that come to ethics committees relate to matters of sexual abuse by male practitioners. Usually these complaints are brought when the practitioner panics and decides to end a relationship which he has realised is foolish or just plain wrong and unethical. Sometimes these cases are brought over matters of incompetent therapy where the practitioner might be able simply to apologise or to refer on to another therapist. What should a therapist do when overwhelmed by feelings of love and desire for a patient? The obvious answer is to consult a senior colleague. This is likely to lead to the advice to terminate the therapeutic relationship as soon as possible which is not easy in the circumstances. The therapist is being advised to give up what she (or more often he) has come to desire very strongly and the patient also at this point may be wanting the relationship to continue with the therapist kept as the idealised father or mother. Ending such a relationship without a great deal of hurt and anger is almost impossible. Some therapists have taken the route of ending the therapeutic relationship: 'I am no longer your therapist, now we can be together'. This is a route that has sometimes been taken although Ethics Committees have seen this solution as little better than continuing and have removed some therapists from licensing. What of the patient who is thus elevated into the position of the therapist's actual partner? Does it spoil the therapy? Is it a form of sexual abuse? In the transference sense in which the therapist is seen as a parent, we would have to suspect that it might be. All the harm that can arise from the parent taking the offspring as a lover may arise. What will certainly arise is the loss of the opportunity to work out the oedipal loss and deprivation of the child who must renounce the parent as lover and find someone else. The therapist has a job to do and this is her ethical responsibility. If she does not continue to do this, she is behaving unethically and is likely to be struck off from the lists of those who may practise.

Continuing the Relationship

Continuing a sexual relationship is unethical for the reasons given above. Sometimes there is pressure to continue with a friendship after the therapy is over. This is not as clearly condemned by the profession but still raises the question of whether the therapy can serve the patient as well in the future if the therapist has abdicated her role and therefore is not seen in the same way. If she is no longer, the neutral interpreting authority, she cannot be used as such in the patient's mind. The inner dialogue in which the ex-patient can ask himself, 'what would X have said about this?' will have to be renounced but maybe adequately replaced by the use of an unconscious good object. By the end of a useful therapy the patient should be able to tolerate the knowledge that his therapist has an ordinary life and does not have any magical ability to avoid problems and disasters. What he will know if she is any good is that she has ways of dealing with what goes wrong for her.

No therapist is likely to remain wholly unknown, even if the patient moves in a different world. In local communities or via the press and the arts, some therapists will be known to their patients to have a life outside their lives as therapists. As early as 1967 Ralph Greenson was pointing out that the full practice of analysis as the provision of a human blank screen on which the patient's transference projections would appear with total clarity was unlikely to be achievable. Is it ethical for the therapist to pursue a second life as a writer or an artist knowing full well that her patients will hear about her? Most therapists have at least one good paper to write and may have to worry about the way in which their patients will receive what they write. There have been cases in which patients recognised their material or thought that they did. We might not be sure whether the ensuing anger is more about the sense of betrayal that the supposed confidential, intimate relationship was actually work to the therapist or more in some cases anger that the therapist did not write about the patient or at least not clearly. Sometimes, the sibling of an abused child is angry that she was not the one chosen.

Publishing material about a patient is well covered in the Ethical Codes of most organisations. There is a variety of different requirements, but written permission is desirable if there is the slightest chance that the patient or anyone else could recognise the material. Even if that is done, is it ethical to use our patients in this way? Some would argue that the profession needs to learn from the work that is done and the patients themselves would suffer if we did not write and publish what we have learned. On the other side of the argument, writing is often partly altruistic in this way and partly narcissistic. The therapist certainly has a clear duty to try to ensure that in meeting her own needs she does not do any foreseeable harm to her patients, present or past.

Money Changes Hands

Patients may often use the idea of the 'professional relationship' as a defence against acknowledging their loving or hating feelings for their practitioner. It is true that the professionalism of the practitioner is of immense importance and is emphasised by the payment of a fee. Patients are often suspicious of the practitioner who does not charge or does not charge enough. They are rightly inclined to wonder 'what does she want from me if not money?' and a much more difficult transference to the mother who wants your life or the father who wants your body may emerge. This will also be useful of course if the practitioner is able and willing to interpret it.

Therapists in private practice and in some of the voluntary sectors charge fees or contributions. Those working for insurance companies or in the State or Corporate sector generally will not. In both cases there are ethical questions in relation to what the therapist wants from the patient. The patient's expectation of what this might be is usually revealed at the very beginning. Some think that any fee set is much more than they can manage to pay from their depleted resources. Such a patient might also have a high level of envy of the parent who is seen as having everything already and not being in need of his hard earned treasure. On the other hand, the patient who has achieved a working false self in Winnicott's sense (1960) will offer to pay whatever is asked and may even offer more if the fee is negotiable.

Money of course plays a major role in the understanding of transference. Neville Symington (1986) saw it as part of his own transference to his patient the purest form of *counter-transference*. When he was seeing a woman who could not pay very much, he allowed her to pay him a reduced fee. He discovered eventually that he saw her as 'poor Ms X', so that when he was increasing his fees on his annual cycle he always assumed that she would not be able to pay him any more. She seemed not to be making any progress. With the insight that occasionally comes to us, Symington understood that his expectation of this patient was very low and that this was holding her back. He decided to raise her fee and did so. As a result his patient seems to have responded to the greater faith in her that her analyst had achieved and he was able to believe more in herself and her own potential.

Payment is part of the way in which as human beings we manage our relationships. Those who provide therapy free of charge are being paid by someone else and are seen to be providing either charity or simply 'doing a job'. Patients will make something of this scenario in the terms of their own transference. At one pole will be the demand: 'I pay my taxes, make me better'. At the other end is the shame: 'You must have many people who need you more than I do'.

The payment of a reasonable fee is perhaps some sort of acknowledgement that the relationship must remain professional in spite of the power of the emotions and the energy that they will generate. It also helps to even out the inequality of the situation in which one is the therapist/one who knows and the other is the vulnerable, needy patient who is at her mercy. Psychoanalysts traditionally also use formal titles even while encouraging their patients to lie down. The hope is that 'Mrs Smith' will lie on the couch and regress to some of her infantile states that are causing her problems. At the same time, both are reminded that she is not that child but a mature adult with a title and a place in the world and the ability to pay something for her therapy. The counsellors on the whole do not follow this tradition and the psychotherapists are divided: some do and some do not.

Carl Rogers promulgated three core conditions which set out the ethical principles for person centred therapists. These are summed up as attention to:

- Empathy
- Genuineness
- Respect.

As a statement of general ethical principles from which codes of practice can be derived, they are of use to all psychological therapists including those of the analytic schools. Genuineness and respect must form part of the therapeutic relationship for most therapists. The use of empathy is partly a technical matter and varies in the degree of emphasis that is given to it at least in its articulation by the therapist. Within these parameters there can be much variation in the way in which they are put into practice but there can be no variation in the need to give a service which puts the welfare of the patient first and which seeks to find the truth in all its forms as best it can be seen.

Conclusion

The analytic therapist will always be in a position of power and will have to withstand all the temptations of being in a room alone with a patient. It is notoriously difficult for a patient to prove that the therapist caused him harm. This makes it even more imperative for the therapist to behave ethically and never to lapse into 'just this once' or 'this patient needs me to behave in an unusual (unethical) way'. The vast majority of therapists have been so well trained that they would never knowingly put a patient at risk. This chapter has made clear that there are many situations in which the ethical path may not always be illuminated or signposted and the therapist has to fall back on her ability to think through the situation from her principles.

Discussion Points

1. A young woman aged 24 has come to see a therapist complaining of loneliness and a lack of self worth. After the first month of weekly sessions she says that she is feeling better. The therapist then tells her that she is going to be away for a month's holiday in two weeks. She feels bad about not having told the patient earlier but was waiting for her to 'be more settled in the therapy'. The patient returns to the next session and says that she feels no better in fact she feels worse and that she intends to go home and take an overdose. She says that she has a large cache of sleeping pills that she has been saving. She gets up and walks out of the session early.

    a. The therapist does not have permission to contact anyone. What should she do?

2. When should the therapist contact a doctor without the patient's permission?
3. Should the therapist be friendly and welcoming at the first meeting?
4. How important is the fee in the therapeutic relationship?

8 Can You Teach and Learn to Practise Therapy Through the Use of Transference?

Questions to consider while reading:

1. What can the concept of transference tell us about the process of training?
2. What can a trainee and a trainer or supervisor make of their understanding of transference?
3. When is it not appropriate to interpret transference in the training context?

Introduction

Since transference patterns are a fundamental building block in the human psyche no-one is exempt from their effects. Training is a hot bed of emotion because people are experiencing for the first time what it means to suffer from the problems of their patients in the new and disciplined way that is required of them in the role of therapist rather than relative, friend or colleague. Anxiety is particularly prevalent although I have seen whatever pathology was originally present in the person appearing to alarming degrees in the training process. Training staff, including supervisors and teaching staff have their own anxieties about allowing people to qualify in this profession in which they will be affecting people's minds for good or ill and over a long period. At every level, transference patterns will appear in their defensive role to protect each person against the anxiety of their role in the process. This chapter will examine what this might mean for both trainees and staff as they struggle to enable good therapists to emerge into the world of responsible and effective clinicians.

Transference for Trainees in Training

I shall refer to those training in both counselling and psychotherapy courses as *trainees*. They wear metaphorical white robes (the literal meaning of *trainee* was *one wearing a white robe*) showing that they are not yet independent practitioners.

Transference as this book so far has demonstrated is a complex concept which in part explains the way in which human minds work. It is not unique to the practice of psychological therapy but one of the tasks of psychological therapy is to discover what kind of transference affects each individual. The popular use of the term to mean 'damaging attachment to the therapist' may be a definition which is initially shared by the trainee. The intention of this book is to show everyone who reads it that the practice of therapy implies something much more complex and imposes a responsibility to understand what power the therapist may appear to possess and to use it wisely.

The concept of transference is essential to someone who is training to use analytic therapy and also to those who are doing the teaching. If, as I have argued in previous chapters, transference provides a way of thinking about human behaviour that has validity and is useful in understanding what impels a particular form of behaviour, then we would expect to find it in all human relationships. There is no reason to think that we ever get beyond the stage of seeing through a transferential filter. Analytic training requires that the therapist has a personal therapy and is able to use the tools of analysis to work out what she might be transferring from her past in a particular situation or with a particular person. We require that the trainers and supervisors of future therapists, let alone the training therapists have a better understanding of themselves and their own transference potential than the trainee in training. Nevertheless, the trainee is also required to be making an effort to learn to use transference and to try to understand what is happening to him or to her in analytic terms.

Ultimately the trainee will qualify and that demands some resolution of the idealising or destructive transference which has set the training staff apart from those whom they train. An enforced resolution with a move towards independence will have to take place for the trainees. This too can be a learning experience for them if the staff can handle its vicissitudes with understanding.

Why does Anyone want to be a Therapist?

This is an important question for all trainees and potential trainees to ask themselves. Conscious answers spring to mind about the wish to help people as well as a fundamental interest in people. Often, the applicant will say that she likes listening to people and has been told that she is good at it. She may occasionally have a particular world view such as a religious conviction that she wishes to convey to others. Some of these motives will be found insufficient or inappropriate in the selection process. These people will not be selected for training. Some inappropriate motives will survive in the mind of the person who enters into the training process. On the other hand, the desire to learn about human nature and the interest in how the human mind works will take a trainee through the requirements of the training and subsequent working life. What the interviewers must consider is the preformed transference of the trainee to the work of analysis and to the profession of counselling or psychotherapy. Both trainee and staff will be aware of the reputation of the profession and of the specific training institution. The trainee will transfer some past experience into his reaction to the reputation and will not necessarily be aware of what part this plays. Articulating the unconscious motivation should be the task of the training therapist but some courses do not require therapy to take place before the course begins. In this situation the trainee may not have been asked to consider what her deeper patterns of response might be.

Each trainee will have brought emotional responses from the past that might make this a desirable profession. If these transferred desires are not examined they could trip her up in the future.

Ms J applied to a three year Diploma course in psycho-dynamic counselling at a university in her town. She did not have a particular reason for choosing that course other than that it was near to her home. She has suffered from severe depression and had seen a counsellor for six months before the counsellor left the area. She had greatly admired the counsellor and felt that she would like to help people in that way. The first year of the course was easy for her and she passed the essays and seemed confident in the role play sessions. In the second year she was required to have some personal therapy and to begin seeing a client. She did not wish to have therapy again and thought that it would confuse her if she were to be both a client and a counsellor at the same time.

She arrived at her first session with one of the recommended counsellors in a very angry mood. 'The bus didn't come and then I had forgotten which turning to take to get here. It will be very difficult to come at this time.' 'Yes' said the therapist. 'You told me it was not the right time for you to begin therapy' 'That was not what I meant.' Ms J was angry with her previous counsellor for leaving and seemed to hope that by becoming her own therapist in a sense, she would avoid the painful feelings of loss and abandonment that she was experiencing. Beginning to work with another therapist merely made the loss more noticeable and for the first few sessions prevented anything except various forms of acting out of anger and resentment. The therapist was in a difficult position. If the client continued in this refusal to examine her own feelings, how could she be allowed to work with the clients that she was planning to begin seeing in a local bereavement service? Should she tell the Course Manager about her concerns?

The therapist decided to ask Ms J whether she thought she was ready to begin seeing clients. She replied that she was. She said that many people had told her she was a good listener and during the course she had been able to help several of her colleagues with good advice. 'Also, 'she added as an afterthought, 'My older sister would never listen to me. I have always wanted someone to listen to me'. Then she looked embarrassed and said 'I mean, I have always wanted to listen to other people'. The therapist was very interested by this slip. 'Perhaps you were right in both of those things? You did want someone to listen to you and you hope that the clients will love you and listen to you in the way that did not happen at home?' Ms J became enraged by this question and said 'That does it. You don't understand me and you never will. I am leaving now.' She walked out of the session and left the training course. The therapist was relieved not to have to solve her reporting dilemma but at the same time was very concerned for Ms J. There was no opportunity to work further with the confused motivation and the way in which the transference had intervened in it. Perhaps, if she could have stayed, she could have recognised it sufficiently to be able to continue to train and to see clients without harming them through the intensity of her own needs.

This case illustrates the degree of responsibility held by therapists who work with trainees and the difficulty of carrying out that responsibility when training courses send trainees for therapy seeing it as a minor adjunct to the other elements of the training rather than seeing it as the central and most important part of the training. Yet even with a most thorough analysis and a highly committed trainee it is not always possible to discover and analyse the most deeply rooted unconscious motivation for doing this work. An awareness and acceptance of this limitation in oneself will also be an important part of the training.

Can You Teach Anyone to be a Therapist?

Freud did not believe that there is such a thing as a person who is completely analysed. Being *completely analysed* would in Freudian theoretical terms mean that the unconscious had become completely conscious. We can scarcely imagine what that would mean in terms of a human being. Without a source of unconscious phantasy, perhaps there could be no dreams. Without a place to put our wishes, we would have to carry our unacceptable desires and feelings around with us all the time. Without a source of unconscious phantasy we might not have to develop behaviour that feels inexplicable. We would never feel the need to say 'I don't know what came over me' or 'I don't know what possessed me to do that'. These common expressions convey the popular awareness of the universality of extrusions from the unconscious which the conscious mind does not recognise as belonging to the subject or the 'I'.

The business of training sets up a division between those who are in authority, the ones who know and those who come to learn from them. Students in ancient and mediaeval universities came and sat in front of the 'chair' and listened to the person who sat in it. Those who were seeking academic knowledge and an academic career were required to defend a thesis which was put to them on the day and which they had not been able to prepare. The trainee had to use his wits as well as his knowledge. The vast majority of the population were most unlikely to be able to attend a university in Europe or North America until the twentieth century opened up the academic qualifications as an alternative to the apprenticeship model of training by which crafts were taught. This is a model of learning which can, in my experience, encourage idealisation and the charismatic teacher may attract and retain students through the power of his or her personality. There is clearly a temptation for the practical role of therapist to be learned purely by imitation of the trainee's own therapist. Fortunately, psychotherapy is taught and passed on from generation to generation by a mixture of the academic and apprenticeship models. Trainees have to demonstrate to their supervisors that they have mastered basic skills and techniques through working with patients and they must defend their model of working in a written thesis or qualifying paper. This mixed model of education has implications for teachers and supervisors and for those who learn from them.

Psychotherapy presents some difficulties in terms of the way it is taught or indeed in whether it can be taught at all. There is certainly a body of knowledge making up the theory of psychoanalysis but the process by which someone becomes able to help another human being who is suffering from emotional distress is not easy to define or to demonstrate. Some of the analytic training schools have taken ideas from the founder of the counselling movement in the United States. In the 1960's Carl Rogers and some educational theorists turned traditional education on its head, asserting robustly that there is no such thing as teaching, only learning. The psychoanalytic establishment has been variably responsive to the implications for training its future psychotherapists and psychoanalysts. Jacqueline Rose in her incisive examination of the question of training for psychoanalysis (2000) argues that the success of teaching in psychoanalysis has to be measured by its failure. Failure in this context means that if it were to pass on exactly what the teacher knows, the work would die. It must grow and change with each generation and with each new patient. This paradox arises because passing on an accurate imitation of the existing practice cannot be all that happens if we take as our aim the encouragement of a new generation of creative and vigorous analysts who are not merely clones of the previous generation. Such analysts will not meekly accept the teaching of the older generation and any attempt to make them comply will fail. Patterns of learning style and of attitudes to authority will affect the process from the beginning. Rose quotes Mustapha Safouan who argues that what he sees as 'the failure' of the International Psychoanalytic Association must be ascribed to its success in propagating itself down the generations (2000: 9).

Clearly this statement arises from the position that learning a theoretical model and a body of techniques will in itself prevent the development of new and iconoclastic ideas. This can hardly be the whole truth or we would have to assume that, for example, Carl Jung would not have been able to find the creativity to challenge Freud's ideas if he had thoroughly understood them. In fact, the opposite is true. He had to grasp Freud's ideas in order to depart from them Of course each of the main figures of analytic theory who have succeeded Freud brought some ideas which came from their own history and experience and some ideas which were a response to Freud. Many of his followers certainly had a view of Freud which was to some extent parental. Ernest Jones is described in the biography by Brenda Maddox as feeling hero worship of Freud and longing to be seen as his son (2007). This attitude to a teacher is useful up to a point but brings with it the inherent risk that the son will have to rebel against the father and take over his role. Freud's own theory predicts that this will happen. and in the case of his own followers, the most devoted were the most likely to separate painfully.

The essential premise of Freud's view of psychoanalytic technique is that it works through one person's unconscious listening to that of another and both have to become conscious in order to achieve control for the ego. Unlike Hamlet, we must be willing to make ourselves into pipes to be played upon by the unconscious of the patient. How can a trainee make herself into a more sensitive pipe? The answer for anyone who imbibes Freud's theory must lie in better tuning the practitioner's sensitivity to receive what can emerge from the unconscious. In most European and American countries, analytic training is based on a university degree which may be in a related but different subject such as psychology or medicine as well as in the subject itself. How does an academic training prepare a practitioner to work in the clinical setting where she is attempting to change people's minds? Not everyone would agree that the work requires a high level of intellectual ability. A sort of well honed worldly wisdom might perhaps be enough.

The history of this model of training began with Freud who analysed his trainees himself in the early days up to about 1923. Safouan points out that Freud adjusted this analysis according to the neurosis of his patient but kept it 'absolutely free from interference by administrative rules and political considerations' (2000: 58). Freud was not even willing to insist that everyone must have a training or 'didactic' analysis. Safouan quotes Siegfried Bernfeld as having been told by Freud that he should just go right ahead and if he got into trouble Freud would see what he could do to help him (ibid.) The new analysts themselves however felt in need of thorough analysis. The group of analysts who were establishing themselves in Berlin all knew each other and therefore they invited Hans Sachs from Vienna to come to Berlin to conduct their analyses. He did so and began the tradition of separating the teaching of theory both from the analysis itself and from the supervision of clinical work (the control analysis). He did this by teaching in seminars in which all the analysts could participate. There must have been some fairly complex sibling transferences in such a situation but it was certainly the origin of the idea that analysis should be separated from teaching and from supervision.

Passing on Patterns or Breaking Moulds

One of the problems inherent from the very beginning of psychoanalytic training (which is a much broader matter than the training of psychoanalysts) has been the question of authority. Who
has the authority to authorise the practice of a new psychoanalyst, psychotherapist or counsellor? The training schools in practice do take this authority. Freud's first analysts had to promise
that they would not begin to practise analysis until authorised
to do so by the institute. This meant that the analyst of the
trainee would be asked whether and when the trainee was ready
to begin. It was not until 2001 that Otto Kernberg made some
clear and firm statements about the mixture of actual power
and transferential power that this situation evoked. He said that
in his view training analysis should be separate from teaching
and supervising and that appointment to each of these positions
should be awarded on the grounds of merit and ability rather
than on the grounds of seniority and the power to command.
He went on to seek to moderate the authority of the training
analysts with a proposal to empower the trainees themselves:

> Trainees' organisations should have a specific role in evalu-
> ating the educational process, providing a structure for the
> redress of grievances and participating in the administrative
> functions in the Institute at all levels.   (Kernberg 2001)

Kernberg also has had much to say about the nature and quality of the teaching that is desirable for trainees. Although he
speaks of psychoanalysis, he advocates a broad view and a generous attitude to other approaches than one's own. Patterns are
also important to therapists in other schools even though they
may use other terminology to describe them e.g. 'schemas' in
Cognitive Behaviour Therapy. Therefore seminar leaders should
be chosen for their ability to convey the 'richness and variety'
of the field. They should be able to stimulate questions and
encourage research. Such an attitude is far from a rigid transmis-
sion of received truths. Research has not figured very largely in
counselling and psychotherapy training outside the universities
although clinical effectiveness and outcome research are increasingly recognised as relevant to public accountability especially if

public funding or insurance is in question. Some of the training schools are recognising the importance of this aspect of education and are setting out to teach research awareness as well as to encourage the undertaking of research degrees. Trainees for training are sometimes motivated by a desire to help others and they wish to do this by a caring, loving approach. Convincing the new student that she needs to use her mind and her ability to weigh evidence as well as her wish to do good is not always easy.

What are the training schools to do? They can either rigorously maintain the existing patterns of thinking and behaving or they can encourage and allow new and creative departures from them. If they are based in a university they will be required to spell out learning outcomes. If they are not connected to a university, they may use a very vague set of criteria open to subjective opinions and unreliable interpretation of standards to be operated by those who have been given this authority. Some of the complaints and appeals that come to the registering bodies focus on this lack of criteria or the lack of clarity about what they are. On the other hand, we are dealing with a profession in which originality of thought and creativity is valued. These must be tempered by strong ethical training and by a certainty that the practitioner will do no harm.

We might all agree that this kind of safety needs to be part of any training. In addition to this minimum, Jacques Lacan on the other hand was very clear that you need a well prepared unconscious and that is very different from requiring a professional who has merely passed exams in a body of theory or even one who has been observed applying techniques safely. In order to do that, one could take an admired teacher as a model and internalise what he or she shows to be good practice. As far as it goes, that can be useful but it is also limiting:

> I have never spoken of the formation [training] of analysts. What I have spoken of are the formations of the unconscious. There is no analytic training. Out of analysis an experience evolves which it is a complete mistake to classify as didactic. Experience is not didactic.   (Lacan, 1973: 121)

I take this to be the argument against the possibility of training in analytic work that does not include analysis. It is also an argument for breaking existing transference patterns. On the other hand, it is not clear that other aspects of training are not also helping the trainee to learn about her own unconscious. For example, some training programmes include an experiential group and in this setting the unconscious emerges powerfully, both for the individual and for the individual as related to others. A group will also demonstrate to the trainee in training the power of transference in that she will be able to begin to see how her projections onto other members of the group portray her own history. This sort of experience can be of immense value in coming to understand the power of her own unconscious processes in the interpretative presence of a qualified group therapist.

Oedipus in Training

In training there are many triangular patterns in which the existence of a third term in the oedipal equation of two parents plus a child will compel the trainee to deal with a fully evolved oedipal question. The pairing provided by the training therapy is interrupted just as the parental mother or father plus baby is interrupted by the other parent. There is a supervisor. The training supervisor is a figure of immense potential authority, quite capable of sharing the transference to the analyst and the institution. Training revives the most difficult phase of the oedipal situation. There is an intense and highly charged partnership between the therapist in training and the analyst. In a training group, much of the energy centres round the rivalry of the siblings over their analytic parents. Rose (2002) points out that it is hardly surprising that institutions based on these dyads have difficulties in functioning well as a large group. Yet there are third terms that intervene for all trainees at some point. There are the founding fathers and mothers such as Freud himself, Klein or Lacan and the trainee may feel a need to identify herself with a school to an extent that she experiences her attachment to a theoretical model as if it were an emotional attachment to a parent who must not be threatened in the playground by any cries of 'My Dad is bigger than your Dad'.

Such attachments are of course much less likely in the schools that encourage critique. Certainly the universities are requiring the schools that are offering academic qualifications to require comparison, contrast and critique to an extent that will make the single model school more difficult to maintain. This will not prevent individuals from finding that a particular theoretical approach evokes the parent in either a positive or negative sense.

Transference of Humility

The process of training in any profession is likely to rekindle the experiences that the child has had with the adult who knows better. Psychotherapy is a craft as well as an art and a science. Trainees learn their craft from their experience under supervision, from their own experience in role play and from their reading and understanding of theory and technique. Most of all they learn from a training analysis. These experiences and the trainee's response to them will provide an excellent opportunity for the new psychotherapist to be humbled by the knowledge that her own conscious experience is the tip of an iceberg whose depths will always remain hidden. Transference of past experience is of the utmost importance in the training of psychotherapists and counsellors One of the many reasons why a period of analysis is essential for anyone who is going to practise this profession which has emotional dangers for therapist as well as patient, is that he and she must discover the nature of their own predominant transferences in order to understand how they will respond to patients who will activate what lies hidden and often the most difficult parts of what lies hidden. The power and conviction carried by the patterns from the past must be felt in order to be believed and must be felt to enable a trainee to establish empathy with the pain and suffering that the patients may bring. The psychotherapist or counsellor who goes into the work with a purely intellectual knowledge of such matters will be a dangerous practitioner with no clear and personal knowledge of how much transference can matter. Only personal experience can teach the vulnerability and humility that a practitioner needs.

Of course there is no guarantee that the experience of training will teach anything at all. Training is a necessary, but not a sufficient, condition for becoming an effective and ethical practitioner. In my role in a training organisation and also sitting on ethics committees I have encountered training analysts who seem not to see how their own transference to the trainee is potentially damaging. This betrays itself in the tendency to give advice or to make statements that can be heard as advice. When a trainee says 'My analyst says I should go to supervisor 'y' or 'my therapist says 'I should transfer to a different training' we might not always believe that there has been such a bald piece of advice as the trainee suggests, but there has probably been a statement which depended on the unanalysed parental transference for its force. From outside the consulting room, one can rarely know enough to judge others definitively, but the need for a clear understanding of the power of transference in us all is undeniable. If a training analyst has not had her own transference patterns carefully analysed she is unlikely to be able to help the trainees who come to her to discover and identify unconscious material. Fortunately, in training, there are other opportunities for this to happen so that even if a training therapy turns out to be less than sufficiently rigorous, the trainee may still be helped by a group conductor or a seminar leader who is able to see what is happening and has the courage and the skill to deal with it appropriately.

How can trainers tell when the trainee is developing the ability to understand transference? As far as the training institute is concerned, it is very difficult to know whether the process towards self knowledge is happening satisfactorily except through the reports of the clinical work. Jürgen Korner tackled the question of the didactics of psychoanalytic education. Jürgen Korner (2002) says that it is very difficult to define this developmental process, let alone say whether it has happened. The training analysis or therapy is of the utmost importance but in all other professions, we expect practitioners to have a knowledge of the theory that is certified by the education or training institutions. All training includes seminars where theory is discussed and often also includes experiential groups which might give an opportunity to analyse the transference to the training institution itself. Korner addresses the triangular nature of the relationships that are set up in the training process. There is a relationship between the teacher and the trainee and there is a relationship between each one and the subject matter. The subject matter has some parameters which can be defined. For example, the future counsellor, psychotherapist or psychoanalyst needs to know the theoretical basis of the model or models that she intends to practise. She needs to know a great deal of the anecdotal literature on which the theory is largely based. This is in principle an intellectual process and would have testable, examinable results. But we know that an examination of this knowledge might give us some useful information about the knowledge of the potential therapist but leaves out the most crucial question of the way in which this knowledge can be used. Examinations or at least regular papers that are marked for theoretical knowledge and accuracy can complement the clinical work and show how the trainee is dealing with her transference to authority in the present.

Transference to the Theory

We can also, Korner suggests, teach application of theory to practice through such methods as supplying clinical material which stops after a statement by the patient. He would then ask the trainees what they would say to the patient. This is a valuable teaching tool. It is open to distortion through transference to the seminar leader whose own view of what is appropriate may not be stated directly but will come across indirectly and will have an effect, whether the trainees respect his or her ability and choose to identify or to rebel against it. There will also be a group view which may emerge in a unified form or may be split but which is likely to influence the individual trainee in ways which will be determined by his or her transference to the group.

When we reach this point in thinking about the training process, we inevitably arrive at a point where transference can be seen to play a part in all the processes of training. If this is the case, the word can lose all useful meaning and just be an alternative word for 'attitude'. In fact, the term *transference* is most useful when there are difficulties. When a trainee shows a particular liking for a strand of theory or a particular dislike for one model, the trainers may help her to see whether she has brought elements from her past experience with education or with an authority. Telling trainees that all their views and especially all their criticisms are negative transference is not usually helpful even if there is an element of transference. Unless it renders a person unable to hold a reasoned argument or unable to listen to a point of view with due consideration, the trainee's transference is no business of the course. As with transference in the consulting room, interpretation is needed only when the past gets in the way in of the present. The trainee is required to assimilate a coherent strand of theory and to apply it to her practice with her patients. The attitude to the theory will of course vary from one person to another and will contain in it something of the trainee's experience of authority. The process of training is, like the process of therapy a slow movement through various degrees of dependency towards increased autonomy and independent functioning. The intention of the teacher, like that of the therapist must be to become redundant but to have made a difference. The difference may not be consciously recognised or measured but it will constitute a change which we might think of as structural. The trainee who learns to think of development and mental functioning in terms of the paranoid schizoid and depressive positions is likely to use these concepts to form a template for examining her own functioning as well as that of her patients. In taking on this theoretical conceptualisation, she is also likely to be accepting some dependency on Klein and on her whole body of theory. In doing so, there will be some transferred feelings about the role of the mother. For some there is a guilty triumph in letting mother be more important than Freud, the founding father.

When the State enters the scene, as it does in countries that have adopted state regulation, it tends to attract parental transference and be seen as either the father who demands discipline or the parent who provides everything. In either case, the responsibility of the individual may be diminished. Korner points out that the state regulation of training in Germany has led to a decrease in the psychoanalytic content of the training and an increase in what he calls the *psychotherapeutic* content (2002: 1399). Regulation makes some difficulties for the aspects of the education of a future practitioner that cannot easily be defined or measured. Assessment of the future clinician is dealt with in varying ways across the profession but is usually a matter mainly of supervisor's reports.

The whole process of assessment has in some cases been secretive and highly authoritarian according to some of the cases that are brought to ethics committees for consideration. This has partly been an effect of the subversive nature of the origins of psychoanalysis. Freud and his immediate followers had to battle against the forces of complacency in bourgeois society. These forces expressed themselves in a reluctance to acknowledge the power of the unconscious. Those who feel a strong bond of common purpose because they are fighting against the general views of society are likely to be cautious in allowing other people to join them. This sense of common purpose could lead to the most senior members of societies taking it upon themselves to make assessment decisions based largely upon subjective views of trainees' ability. The trainees themselves need to have knowledge of the reasons for the assessment decisions that are made, especially when there is a decision to terminate or prolong training. Decisions that are based on clear and explicit criteria give protection against the effect of the trainers' transference to the trainees. Once again, the universities are having a very positive effect in their requirement for clear learning outcomes. Open ended outcomes can encourage creativity and need not be constricting but do require clear thinking about how to express what is needed in a safe clinical practitioner. A training programme that has university validation as a master's degree or doctorate will need transparent criteria and procedures.

Who Decides that the Trainee is Ready to Practise?

In most traditional training, the supervisors hold the power to put a trainee forward for qualification or to prevent it. The structure usually involves a supervisor reporting to a Training Committee which will consist of some of the most experienced and knowledgeable senior members of the organisation. In most cases, the Training Committee takes the ultimate responsibility for deciding whether or not a trainee is ready to qualify but the decision will usually be based on the evidence obtained from the supervisor who is the only person apart from the patient who knows what the standard of the work has been. In the supervisory relationship there is all the power of the parent on one side and in most cases, however much the two are able to work co-operatively on understanding the needs of the patient, the time will come when the supervisor has to take the responsibility for the final decision. This has various potential difficulties arising from the transference in the relationship. The supervisor may respond to the trainee as if to a child. Harold Searles described his own experience of the patient as his 'oedipal love object' (1986). He very honestly asserted that the patient could fulfil for him the role of the desired and needed object which might be the parent or might be the child in transference terms. The supervisee can also play this role for the supervisor and depending on his own oedipal experience in the past, he will want to please or impress his supervisee or will want revenge for the past wrongs that he considers were done to him by his father or even in some cases the wrongs done by the son or daughter who has not been grateful enough.

Supervisors have the same difficulties in dealing with the transference in the training relationship as therapists have with their patients. On the other hand, they are usually the most experienced members of the profession and therefore have the tools to deal with their own feelings. They will need to accept the loss of the person whom they are allowing to qualify and finish the training. They will need to deal with the narcissistic wound of allowing the analytic son or daughter to grow up and go out into the world to become perhaps more successful or more respected than they are. At the very least they will lose the esteem and admiration which trainees can give to their training supervisors who hold the authority of a parental position. The parental nature of the relationship has to be dissolved and the supervisor has to allow the trainee to become a colleague. In many cases the training supervisor continues to supervise the trainee's work after she qualifies. This is partly a matter of convenience and continuity but may also be partly an effect of the power of the transference pattern.

Some training organisations have tried to minimise the impact of this parental transference in the training process. In the UK, the Cambridge Society for Psychotherapy and the Site for Contemporary Psychoanalysis for example, consist of a training group in which all trainees take part together in the teaching and discussion of the teaching. A trainee must decide for herself that she is ready to qualify and leave the group. This is not as easy as it sounds. In practice, it is very difficult to say to colleagues that one is ready for independent practice and in fact also ready to leave the training group to which each trainee has become attached. Colleagues can be hard task masters, often demanding a great deal although this process, as I have seen it, is usually done with care and consideration for each individual. Envy and rivalry naturally play a part in these training groups but the group is always aware that each person will be in this position at some point and therefore the negative emotions tend to be kept sufficiently in check to enable the group to function most of the time as a working group.

While supervisors must have a final veto over the quality of the trainee's work, there are some benefits for the trainee in having to make his or her own decision about readiness to qualify without recourse to a superior authority. A qualified counsellor or psychotherapist will have many decisions to make about what is helpful to another person. The person who cannot decide that she is ready to take that responsibility is unlikely to be ready for the kind of work that she will be doing. Usually the supervisor will still have an important part to play and may intervene if she thinks that the trainee is definitely not ready but would not usually deprive the trainee of the opportunity to say for herself that she *is* ready. A trainee in training who has been able to authorise herself to be ready to begin to practise is making a great advance towards dissolving the transference to the training organisation and to the supervisor and possibly to the therapist. She still has to be willing to think about her transference to the founding fathers and mothers. Resolution of transference is always a difficult concept to define. A resolution implies that the desire for and the fear of the authority of the other are both moderated and that neither interferes too much with the relationship. From the point of view of the graduate, the training organisation becomes, like the parents, a mixture of good and bad and is able to be experienced as having been imperfect but not totally bad. This is difficult to achieve given that there will have been usually some judgment of the trainee's fitness to practise and that judgement always enhances the parental nature of a role. Maturity and the trainee's own analysis may enable the judgment to be accepted and the lessons learned without too much resentment and anger remaining. Like the parents, the training organisation can lose its archaic power and be merely a place that was helpful in the past.

Conclusion

This chapter has looked at the way in which the operation of patterns must affect the patient and also the therapist at every level and at every stage of development. If we accept that transference is a useful concept for working with patients, we must also accept that it will affect our own perceptions. Seeing and understanding how this works difficult, if not impossible, for the inexperienced trainee but should be a requirement for those who are teaching and supervising. They must be the most experienced and thoughtful practitioners and therefore have the obligation to consider their own part in the process, resisting temptation to blame the trainees, encouraging debate and questioning even when that debate impinges on the admiration and respect for the parental theorists and supervisors in the teacher's own mental functioning.

If we can establish the value of scrutinising all that we do and say as practitioners, seeking out our own patterns of response to consider whether or not they are appropriate to the present. The blind man making his way round the obstacles in his room needs to learn the pattern but if the obstacles are moved to a completely different pattern or are removed altogether in the present, he will be much better off if he can respond to what is the new truth for him. Understanding transference is all about seeking the truth. Self deception is something that we all do very well but the task of analytic therapy is to help us to struggle to find and live by the truth as best we can. Seeing and understanding patterns is a skill for the therapist and becomes a life long quest for us and for the patients whom we seek to help.

Discussion Points

A trainee in training complains to the Training Committee that her supervisor is not giving her good supervision and she wishes to change to another supervisor. She says that the supervisor is not paying attention to her patients but is talking about his own experience. He does not understand that her patients have specific needs which she herself understands well because she has been through the same things that they are talking about.

1. How can transference help or hinder the training process?
2. How can trainers and supervisors help with transference difficulties without becoming therapists?
3. What would be necessary to enable a trainee to decide that he or she would be ready to quality?

References

Auden, W.H. (2007) *Collected Works*. London: Faber and Faber.

Benvenuto, B. (1986) *The Works of Jacques Lacan: An Introduction*. London: Free Association Books.

Beutel, M. and Rasting M. (2002) 'Long term treatments from the perspectives of former patients' in Bohleber, M. and Target, M. (eds) (2002) *Outcomes of Psychoanalytic Treatment*. London: Whurr.

Bion, W.R. (1955) 'Language and the schizophrenic' in Klein, M., Heimann, P. and Money-Kyrle, R. *New Directions in Psycho-Analysis*. London: Hogarth Press.

Birk, L. (1973) 'Psychoanalysis and behavioural analysis; natural resonance and complementarity'. *International. Journal of Psychiatry*, 11: 160.

Blum, B.R. (1983) 'The position and value of extratransference interpretation'. *Journal of the American Psychoanalytical Association*, 34: 309–28.

Brenman, Pick, I. (1985) 'Working through in the counter-transference'. *International Journal of Psycho-Analysis*, 66: 157–66. A slightly revised version is also published in Spillius, E. Bott (ed.) *Melanie Klein Today*, Vol. 2, *Mainly Practice*. 34–47, London: Routledge,

Britton, R. (1989) 'The missing link: parental sexuality in the Oedipus complex', in Britton et al, *The Oedipus Complex Today*, John Steiner (ed.), 83–101, London: Karnac.

Caper, R. (1998) *A Mind of One's Own*. London: Routledge.

Casement, P. (1985) *On Learning from the Patient*. London: Routledge.

Casement, P. (1990) *Further Learning from the Patient*. London: Routledge.

Casement, P. (2002) *Learning from our Mistakes*. London: Brunner Routledge.

Cavada, C. and Schultz, W., quoted in Schore, A. (2003) in Corrigall, J. and Wilkinson, H. (eds) *Revolutionary Connections*. London: Karnac.

Coren, A. (2001) *Short-term Psychotherapy*. London: Palgrave.

Clark, R. (1982) *Freud: the man and the cause*. London: Paladin.

Coles. P. (2003) *The Importance of Sibling Relationships in Psycho-Analysis*. London: Karnac.

Cremerius, J. (2003) 'Foreword to Caretenuto's *Tagebuch einer heimlichen symmetrie*' in Covington, C. and Wharton, B. (2003) (eds) *Sabina Spielrein*. London: Brunner Routledge.

Cohen, J. (2004) 'On: Institutional responses to boundary violations: The case of Masud Khan'. *International Journal of Psycho-analysis*, 85 (3): 752.

Cooper, J. (1993) *Speak of me as I am: The Life and Work of Masud Khan*. London: Karnac.

Corigall, J. and Wilkinson, H. 2003 *Revolutionary Connections: Psychotherapy and Neuroscience*. London: Karnac.

Covington, C. and Wharton, B. 2003 (eds) *Sabina Spielrein*. London: Brunner Routledge.

Crews, F. (1990) *The Freud Wars*. New York: New York Review Books.

Dalal, F. *Race Colour and Processes of Racialisation*. London: Brunner Routledge.

Dimasio, A. (2000) *The Feeling of What Happens*. London: Vintage.

Dreiser, T. in Clark, R.W. (1982) *Freud: the man and the cause*. London: Paladin.

Fairbairn, W.R.D. (1952) *Psychoanalytic Studies of the Personality*. London: Routledge and Kegan Paul.

Fairbairn, W.R.D. (1952) *Psychoanalytic Studies of the Personality*. London: Tavistock.

Fonagy, P., Kachele, H., Krause, R., Jones, E. and Perron R. (1999) *Open Door Review of Outcome Studies in Psychoanalysis*. London: University College, London.

Freud, S. (1900) '*The Interpretation of Dreams*' in *Standard Edition*. London: Hogarth Press, 4–5.

Freud, S. (1909) 'Analysis of a phobia in a five year old boy' in SE X, 1955.

Freud S. (1912) 'The Dynamics of Transference' SE XII.

Freud, S. (1915) 'Observations on Transference Love' SE XII.

Freud, S. (1915) 'Instincts and their Vicissitudes' SE XIV 109.

Freud, S. (1916) 'Introductory Lectures on Psychoanalysis' SE XVI.

Freud S. (1918) 'From a History of Infantile Neurosis' SE XVII.

Freud, S. (1920) 'Beyond the Pleasure Principle' SE XVlll.

Freud, S. (1925) 'Two Principles of mental Functioning' SE XII.

Freud. S. (1925) 'An autobiographical Study'. London: Hogarth Press.

Frie, R. (2003) *Understanding Experience*. London: Routledge.

Gailard, C. 'Don Quixote in the analyst's consulting room' in Twyman, M and Solomon, H. (eds) (2003) *The Ethical Attitude in Analytic Practice*. London: Free Association Books.

Gerhardt, S. (2004) *Why Love Matters*. London: Brunner Routledge.

Gomez, L. (2005) *The Freud Wars*. London: Routledge.

Gordon, P. (2005) 'Where is the wisdom in the waste' Paper given to the United Kingdom Council for Psychotherapy Ethics Day Conference.

Greenson, R. (1978) *Explorations in Psychoanalysis*. New York: International Universities Press.

Greenson, R. (1985) *The Practice and Technique of Psychoanalysis*. London: Hogarth Press.

Hartley L.P. (1953) *The Go Between*. Harmondsworth: Penguin Books.

Heimann, P. (1950) 'On Counter Transference'. *International Journal of Psycho-Analysis*, 31: 81.

Heimann. P. (1950) 'Dynamics of transference interpretation'. *International Journal of Psycho-Analysis*, 37: 303.

Hinshelwood, R.D. (1994) *Clinical Klein*. London: Free Association Books.

Hinshelwood, R.D. (1997) *Therapy or Coercion?* London: Karnac Books.

Horrocks, R. (2005) *Foundations of Psychotherapy*. London: Palgrave.

Hunter, M. (1997) *The Ethical Use of Touch in Psychotherapy*. London: Sage.

Isroff, R. (1994) 'Becoming a grandmother; the third position'. *British Journal of Psychotherapy*, 11: 2, 260.

Joseph, B. (1989) 'Transference: the total situation' in Feldman, M. and Bott Spillius E. London: Hogarth Press.

Kernberg, O. (2003) 'Convergences and divergences in contemporary psychoanalytic technique'. *International Journal of Psycho-Analysis*, 74: 659.

Kihlstrom, J.F. 2003 'Is Freud still alive? No not really'. This essay was originally prepared for *Hilgard's Introduction to Psychology*, 13th Ed., by R. Atkinson and R.C. Atkinson and was published in revised form in the 14th edition (2003) (quoted in an Internet essay).

Kihlstrom, J. (1987) 'The cognitive unconscious'. *Science*, 237: 1445.

Klein, M. (1952) 'The origins of transference' in Klein, M. (1975) *Envy and Gratitude*. London: Hogarth Press.

Klein, M. (1974) 'The theory of intellectual inhibition' in *Love, Guilt and Reparation*. London: Hogarth Press.

Klein, M. (1975) *Envy and Gratitude*. London: Hogarth Press.

Neuroscience *International Journal of Psychoanalysis*, 86: 5, 1405.

Kőrner, J. (2002) 'The didactics of psychoanalytic education'. *International Journal of Psychoanalysis*, 83: 6, 1395.

Kuhn, T. (1962) *The Structure of Scientific Revolutions*. Chicago: University of Chicago Press.

Knox, J. (2003) *Analytical Psychology: Contemporary Perspectives in Jungian Analysis*. London: Brunner Routledge.

Kohon, G. (ed) (1986) *The British School of Psychoanalysis: The Independent Tradition*. London: Free Association Books.

Kohut, H. (1971) *The Analysis of the Self*. Madison, Conn: International Universities Press.

Lacan, J, (1949) 'Le Stade du miroir comme formateur du fonction du je' *Ecrits* 1966. Paris: Seuil.

Lacan, J. (1977) *Ecrits*, Paris: Seiul.

Laungani, P. (2004) *Asian Perspectives in Counselling and Psychotherapy*. London: Routledge.

Levinas, E. (1996) in Peperzak, A., Critichley, S. and Bernasconi, B. (eds) *Basic Philosophical Writings*. Bloomington: Indiana University Press.

Linehan, M. (1993) Skills Training Manual for treating Borderline Personality Disorder.

Leuzinger-Bohleber, M. (2002) 'A follow up study: critical inspiration for our clinical practice?' in Bohleber M. and Target, M. (eds) (2002) Outcomes of Psychoanalytic Treatment. London: Whurr.

Loewenthal, D. and Snell, R. (2003) *Postmodernism for Psychotherapists* London: Brunner Routledge,

Loftus, E.F., Miller D.G. and Burns J.J. 'Semantic integration of verbal information into visual memory' *Journal of Experimental Psychology, Human Learning and Memory*, 4: 19.

McKenna, C. (2003) 'Ethical Pressures on the analytic alliance' in Smith, E.E., D.J. Bem, and S. Nolen-Hoeksema. New York: Harcourt Brace Jovanovich, 2000.

Maddox, B. (2007) *Freud's Wizard*. London: John Murray.

Malan, D. (1995) Psychotherapy and the Science of Psychodynamics. London: Hodder Arnold.

Mander, G. (1991) 'Some thoughts on sibling rivalry and competitiveness' *British Journal of Psychotherapy*, 7: 4, 368.

Mander, G. (2000) *A Psychodynamic Approach to Brief Therapy*, London: Sage.

Masson J. (1985) *The Assault on Truth*. Harmondsworth: Penguin.

Marks, M. (2002) 'Letting fathers in' in Trowell, J. and Etchegoyen, A. (eds) (2002) *The Importance of Fathers*. London: Brunner Routledge.

Mearns, D. (1997) *Person-Centred Counselling Training*. London: Sage.

Michell, J. (2003) *Siblings*, London: Polity Press.

Money Kyrle, R. (1956) 'Normal counter-transference and some of its deviations' in *The International Journal of Psycho-Analysis*, 37: 360–66. Reprinted in *The Collected Papers of Roger Money-Kyrle* (1978) (ed.), Donald Meltzer with the assistance of Edna O'Shaughnessy, Strathtay, Perthshire: Clunie Press.

Murdin, L. (2000) *How Much is Enough*? London: Routledge.

Murdin, L with Erriington, M. (2005) *Setting Out*. London Routledge.

National Institute for Clinical Excellence (2004) 'Depression: management of depression in primary and secondary care'.

Newman, C. and Goldfried, M. (1996) 'Developments in Psychotherapy Integration' in Dryden, W. (ed.) (1996) *Developments in Psychotherapy*. London: Sage.

New Savoy Declaration (2007) British Psychological Society Website.

Palmer Barnes, F. and Murdin, L. (eds) (2004) *Values and Ethics in Psychotherapy*. Pearson, J. (ed.) 2004 *Analyst of the Imagination* London: Karnac.

Ragland, E. (1995) *Essays on the Pleasures of Death*. London: Routledge.

Roth, A. and Fonagy, P. (2004) *What works for Whom?* London: Guildford Press.

Rosenfeld, H. (1965) *Psychotic States*. New York: International Universities Press.

Rycroft, C. (1968) *A Critical Dictionary of Psychoanalysis*. Harmondsworth: Penguin Books.

Rocchi, C. (2003) 'On the counter transference of the patient'. *Internationalal Journal of Psychoanalysis*, 84: 5, 1221.

Safouan, M. and Rose, J. (2000) *Jacques Lacan and the Question of Psychoanalytic Training*. London: Language Discourse Society.

Samuels, A.,Plaut, F. and Shorter, B. (1986) *A Critical Dictionary of Jungian analysis*. London: Routledge and Keegan Paul.

Samuels, A. (2005) 'Ethics and Diversity' unpublished paper given to WPF Therapy.

Sandler, J. and Fonagy, P. (eds) (1997) *Recovered Memories of Abuse*. London: Karnac.

Sandler, A.M. with Godley, W. (2004) 'Institutional responses to boundary violations'. *International Journal of Psychoanalysis*, 85: 2, 27.

Scalzone, F. (2005) 'Notes for a dialogue between psychoanalysis and neuroscience'. *International Journal of Psycho-Analysis*, 86: 5, 1405.

Schafer, R. (1990) 'The search for common ground'. *International Journal of Psychoanalysis*, 71: 49.

Schore, A. (2003) The Seventh Annual John Bowlby Lecture in Corrigall. J. and Wilkinson, H. (eds) 2000 *Revolutionary Connections* London: Karnac.

Scott, A. (1996) *Real Events Revisited: Fantasy Memory, Psychoanalysis*. London: Virago.

Searles, H. (1986) *Collected Papers on Schizophrenia and Related Subjects*. London: Maresfield.

Shoenberg, P. (2007) *Psychosomatics*. Basingstoke: Palgrave Macmillan.

Spillius, E.Bott (1989) (ed.) *Psychic Equilibrium and Psychic Change*.London: Routledge.

Spillius E. Bott (ed.) (1988) *Melanie Klein Today*, Vol. 2, *Mainly Practice*. London: Routledge.

Sternberg, J. (2005) *Infant Observation at the Heart of Training.* London: Karnac.

Strachey, J. (1934); The nature of the therapeutic action of psychoanalysis'. *International Journal of Psycho-Analysis*, 15, 127–59.

Symington, N. (1986) 'The analyst's act of freedom as an agent of therapeutic change' in Kohon, G. (ed.) (1986) *The British School of Psychoanalysis: The Independent Tradition.* London: Free Association Books.

Twyman, M. and Solomon, H. (eds) (2003) *The Ethical Attitude in Analytic Practice.* London: Free Association Books.

Wallerstein, R. (1989) 'Psychoanalysis and psychotherapy; an historical perspective', *International Journal of Psycho-Analysis*, 70, 563.

Wallerstein, R. (2002) 'The trajectory of Psychoanalysis', *International Journal of Psycho-Analysis*, 83: 6, 1247.

Webster, R. (1995) *Why Freud was Wrong.* London: Harper Collins/Basic Books (US).

White, D. (2008) 'Good going at the Doncaster IAPPT'. *Therapy*, 19: 2, 10.

Whyte, L.L. (1978) *The Unconscious before Freud.* London: Friedmann.

Winnicott, D.W. (1951) 'Transistional objects and transitional phenomena' in 1958 *Through Pediatrics to Psychoanalysis.* London: Karnac Books.

Winnicott, D.W. (1956) 'Letter of 3rd February, 1956 to Joan Riviere' in Rodman, F.R. (ed.) *The Spontaneous Gesture: Selected Letters of D.W. Winnicott.* Cambridge, Mass: Harvard University Press.

Winnicott, D.W. (1960) *The Maturational Process and the Facilitating Environment.* London: Hogarth Press.

Winnicott, D.W. (1964) *The Child, the Family and the Outside World.* Harmondsworth: Penguin Books.

Winnicott, D. (1965) 'Ego distortion in terms of true and false self' in *Maturational Processes and the Facilitating Environment.* London: Hogarth Press.

Winnicott, D. (2006) *The Family and Individual Development.* London: Routledge.

Wolfe, B.F. and Goldfried, M.R. (1988) 'Research on psychotherapy integration: recommendations and conclusions from a NIMHE workshop'. *Journal of Consulting and Clinical Psychology*, 56: 448.

Yelland, I, and Midence, K. 'The role of transference and Counter Transference in the therapeutic relationship within CBT'. *Clinical Psychology Forum*, 179, 7.

Zeal, P. (2006) 'Schreber's Fall'. *British Journal of Psychotherapy*, 22: 4, 449.

Index